Le French
COOKBOOK

Copyright © Bay Books

Published by Bay Books
61–69 Anzac Parade,
Kensington NSW 2033

Publisher: George Barber

National Library of Australia
Card Number and ISBN 1 86256 023 4

BB87

Photography: Ashley Barber

Food preparation and styling: Elizabeth Carden
Photography pages 6–7: Jean-Paul Ferrero,
Auscape International

Le French
COOKBOOK

BAY BOOKS
Sydney and London

Contents

room and Madeira Sauce • Beef Bourguignon • Beef Casserole in Stout • Oxtail Stew • Beef in Red Wine • Veal with Dried Fruits • Blanquette de Veau • Veal with Apple and Calvados • Crumbed Veal Escalopes with Brown Butter • Roast Veal Steaks Parisienne • Lamb and Vegetable Stew • Haricot Bean Lamb Stew • Springtime Saddle of Lamb • Herbed Rack of Lamb • Pot Roast Lamb • Lamb Provençale-style • Pork in Cider • Pork with Rosemary • Pork Crépinettes with Butter-fried Apples • Veal Kidneys in Red Wine • Armagnac Flambéed Kidneys • Sweetbreads in Cream Sauce • Sautéed Chicken with Mushroons • Pan-fried Chicken in Cream Sauce • Chicken Breasts cooked in Green Peppercorns • Roast Chicken with Tarragon • Coq au Vin • Chicken Chaudfroid • Normandy Duck • Duck with Orange • Ballotine of Duck in Red Wine • Braised Quail with Grapes • Quail with Wild Rice • Goose and Mutton Casserole with Haricot Beans •

VEGETABLES   68
Globe Artichokes with Various Sauces • French-fried Asparagus Spears • Asparagus with Hollandaise Sauce • French Beans with Ham, Mushrooms and Tomatoes • Green Beans with Ham • Haricot Beans with French Beans • French-fried Brussels Sprouts • Sautéed Cabbage with Bacon • Braised Red Cabbage with Apples • Raisin-glazed Carrots • Cauliflower with Cheese Sauce • Celery in Rémoulade Sauce • Chicory with Lemon Juice • Eggplant and Tomato Bake • Braised Fennel • Leeks Vinaigrette • Leeks with Egg and Parsley Sauce • Stuffed Mushrooms • Hot Onion Salad • French Peas • Little Peas • Potatoes Boulangère • Duchess Potatoes • Dauphinois Potatoes • Ratatouille • Spinach with Cream • Grilled Tomatoes with Basil Butter • Savoury-filled Tomatoes • Truffles with Butter Sauce • Witlof with Ham • Zucchini with Cream Sauce • Sautéed Zucchini with Parlsey and Garlic Butter •

COLD BUFFET   78
Mushrooms à la Grecque • Crudités • Smoked Eel Salad • Octopus Salad • Roast Beef Salad • Scallop Terrine • Smoked Trout Pâté • Chicken Liver Pâté • Salmon Cream Mousse • Quick Chicken Liver Pâté • Rabbit and Prune Terrine • Mackerel in Spicy Citrus Marinade • Preserved Goose • Breadcases filled with Herbed Snails in Red Wine • Cheese Straws • Prawn Canapés • Cheese Canapés • Paprika Canapés • Avocado Canapés •

DESSERTS AND CAKES   85
Shortcrust Pastry • Choux Pastry • Sweet Flan Pastry • Strawberry Flan • Apple Flan • Caramelised Apple Tart • Pear Tart • Profiteroles and Chocolate Rum Sauce • Croquembouche • Spun Sugar • Pears Belle Hélène • Oranges in Grand Marnier • Meringues in Custard • Strawberry Meringue Gâteau • Crème Caramel • Crème Brûlée • Crème Anglaise • Coeur à la Crème • Grand Marnier Soufflé • Mini Chocolate Pots • Chestnut Bavarois • Chocolate Cointreau Mousse • Caraque • Crêpes Suzette • Apple Charlotte • Rum Babas • Noel Log • Vanilla Ice-cream • Lemon Sorbet •

A TASTE OF FRANCE

France has long been celebrated as the gastronomic centre of the world and, despite the emergence of many other types of cuisine in recent years, we're still inclined to turn to favourite French recipes when in search of a good, dependable dish or looking for a menu with real flair and imagination.

Although French chefs are renowned for their skill and creativity, it is a mistake to confuse the 'haute cuisine' they serve in the country's top hotels and restaurants with the no less tasty traditional fare eaten daily at family tables and bistros around the provinces. Nor can we generalise on the style of French cooking — the vast range of recipes that comes under this heading is, in fact, the product of numerous regions within this primarily agricultural land, each of which has dishes developed from livestock and produce which happens to thrive in that particular area.

Hence we have the marvellous fish dishes of Brittany and the Mediterranean coast, recipes utilising the apple crop in Normandy, the mustard grown around Dijon, paté de foie gras and excellent charcuterie from the goose and pork areas of Perigord and Alsace, while Burgundy and Bordeaux naturally furnish us with a plethora of sauces and casseroles featuring their unbeatable wines.

The French meals we enjoy in restaurants around the world more often find their inspiration in the kitchen of a provincial French housewife than that of a celebrated chef; while we may put escargots de Bourgogne, potatoes Lyonnaise, coq au vin and the enormous range of charcuterie and cheeses on a gastronomic pedestal, we should remember that it is all everyday eating to the French, on par with steak and kidney pie, spaghetti bolognaise, moussaka or even hamburger and chips elsewhere.

The blessing is that, because they are basically quite humble fare, the majority of famous French dishes are easy to shop for and well within the budget of most families.

Haute cuisine at the Hotel de Crillon, Paris

French food is above all, a reflection of the French lifestyle. At midday prompt, shops bring down their shutters, factories grind to a halt, farm workers abandon their fields and all work stops as the nation prepares itself for the day's most serious event so far — le déjeuner. Lunch is not the hasty snack we have come to expect in so many other countries and the reverence with which the French approach even the simplest repast undoubtedly encourages the rest of us to treat their cuisine with enormous respect.

The meal is unquestioningly a sit-down affair lasting several courses starting with, say, a rich homemade terrine followed by a serving of salad, after which there is a main dish such as gigot of lamb, pot au feu or andouiettes. This will be followed by a selection of local cheeses — cheese is *always* eaten before dessert just as vegetables tend to be served separately from the meat dish. The sweet is also likely to be indigenous to the region — perhaps an inviting tarte au pommes or citron. Fresh crusty bread will be passed around the table, served without butter and eaten straight off the cloth. The meal will naturally be washed down with low cost but fair quality wine produced in local vineyards.

Not surprisingly, this marathon takes a good couple of hours and it is well into the afternoon before the espresso coffee is finished, the shops sleepily start re-opening and the streets fill up again. Then, of course, there is the question of le diner, which is likely to be just as much of an occasion as lunch — not surprisingly, statistics reveal that the typical French housewife spends on average three times as long in the kitchen as her counterparts in other parts of the world.

Preparing food and eating it are not the only time-consuming activities for the cook in a French household — shopping for it is an equally serious business. Despite the spread of supermarkets in France, as elsewhere housewives there still cling to their long-standing habit of shopping on a daily basis for food, rather than stocking up for a week or two with convenience products. Freshness and high quality ingredients are vitally important to French cooks, whether the food they are preparing is to be served in a five star hotel or at the family supper table. Few will set out for the market with a determined idea of the dish they will be putting on the table for the midday or evening meal — they are far more likely to be guided by the range and quality of produce available that day.

Street stalls and shops are packed out daily with housewives fastidiously picking over the vegetable selection, questioning the standard of meat or fish and peering closely at the selection of cheeses before making their choice.

Shoppers study a Parisian street stall

Taste, smell and texture are paramount in French cuisine and natural Gallic inquisitiveness and experimentation has led to the creation of some splendidly unusual and imaginative dishes.

But with such an emphasis on the flavour factor, health considerations have, until recently, languished a long way down the list of priorities in French gourmandising. While menus are characterised by a large number of courses rather than over-generous portions, there is no doubt that many traditional dishes have an alarmingly high fat content. Weight problems have not been so great as the risk of heart disease and digestive illness — while France is the jewel in the crown of Europe's kitchens, it is also the home of its most fabled couturiers and most French folk have enough regard for their reputation as incomparably 'chic' to eschew serious gastronomic over-indulgence. However, they are just as prone to the ill-effects of a fat-rich diet as the rest of us.

A French boulangerie

Typically, the French have now contrived a gourmet's solution. It is called 'cuisine minceur' and is effectively an adaptation of traditional dishes and methods of food preparation to incorporate fewer rich and fatty ingredients. The net result is that our favourite French dishes can now be prepared in a way that makes them just as flavoursome but rather less harmful than they are in the traditional recipe.

This departure from standardised cooking styles has proved not only a boon to slimmers and those with a concerned eye on their health, but also to the busy cook. In common with most western cultures, French women are tending to abandon their traditional role in the kitchen and more and more are working outside the home. This has fostered a new interest in innovative recipes which offer corner-cutting time schedules without compromising those all-important flavours.

A smallgoods vendor

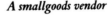

If you're planning to try your hand at creating some authentic French dishes, it makes great sense to have the right tools for the job. This needn't mean a vast expenditure and you will find that certain key items are a wise investment.

Most ingredients in this book are set out in cups and spoons, so for dry ingredients you will need a nest of cups (1 cup, ½ cup, ⅓ cup and ¼ cup) and a set of spoons (1 tablespoon, 1 teaspoon, ½ teaspoon and ¼ teaspoon). For liquids, use a transparent graduated measuring jug (capacity 1 litre or 250 mL).

Another useful buy is a mortar and pestle, which can replace a food processor or blender at a fraction of the price. For sauces, a whisk and a birch brush will banish dismaying lumps, while a length of muslin makes an ideal strainer. A double boiler which provides a barrier between your ingredients and direct heat guarantees better results for sauces and creams.

Many French recipes call for some kind of pastry-making, so you can't automatically escape by using frozen or ready-rolled lengths of pastry.

A rolling pin is an obvious requirement and a pastry brush is a good extra for presentation, as the addition of milk or egg glaze to pies and tarts gives a professional finishing touch.

Metal tartlet cases create an authentic Gallic 'look' for savouries and desserts, and are available in a wide variety of sizes, shapes and designs; it's worth remembering that a small individual tartlet often makes a more visually impressive serving than a single slice from a larger flan.

Presentation is one aspect of French cuisine that can never be overlooked — why diminish a marvellously tasty dish by serving it unimaginatively? Collect a variety of moulds for your pâtés , terrines and jellies — an interesting shape can turn the simplest entrée into a visual feast.

Many utensils vital to French cuisine are universally useful. For instance, you should not do without a pair of tongs for turning cooking food, particularly meat, as tongs will prevent it from being broken, bruised or allowing flavoursome juices to spill out, which is what happens if you make do with a fork. Similarly, good quality knives — those designed with metal running right through the handle — are expertly balanced for chopping, slicing and carving and will generally last far longer than a cheaper style.

Another important culinary aid is a large metal spoon which has many functions, but is especially helpful for jobs like folding in egg whites — the size is important as it allows more air to be incorporated and makes the finished dish lighter. For the same reason, a copper bowl is an ideal medium for *whisking* egg whites.

At a very basic level, a pot stand for hot casserole dishes and saucepans often gives the cook a spare pair of hands, and kitchen string is an essential. Buy only proper fibre string as the synthetic variety melts under heat.

Finally, the escargot holders. These are now available in specialist kitchen stores everywhere and make the fiddly business of extracting those slippery snails from their shells a veritable piece of gateau!

THE SECRET OF THE SAUCES
Le Secret des Sauces

Stocks

BROWN BEEF STOCK
Fond brun

This is a simple, basic brown stock which can be used for brown sauces or soups. The stock can be reserved frozen and used as required. Only use the parsley stalks as the leaves will turn the stock cloudy.

1 kg beef bones
100 g shin of beef
1 onion, chopped
2 litres cold water
1 carrot, chopped
1 leek, washed and sliced
1 bouquet garni
1 teaspoon salt

Place the beef bones and shin in a baking dish with the onion and bake at 180°C (350°F) for 45 minutes or until well browned. Turn the onion occasionally to prevent burning.

Strain and discard any fat from the pan and transfer the bones and onion to a large, straight-sided saucepan. Add the remaining ingredients and bring to the boil, skimming off any foam that may rise to the top.

Reduce the heat and simmer, covered for 4–5 hours, occasionally skimming the surface.

Strain the stock and leave to cool. When cold, refrigerate for several hours. Skim off any fat that may form on the top and use stock as required.
Makes about 1.5 litres

WHITE STOCK
Fond blanc de veau

1 kg raw knuckle of veal, chopped
2 litres cold water
juice ½ lemon
½ teaspoon salt
1 onion, chopped
1 carrot, chopped
1 bouquet garni
1 teaspoon salt
6 peppercorns

Wash the veal bones, then put them in a large straight-sided saucepan with the water and lemon juice. Bring to the boil and skim off any foam or fat that rises to the surface.

Add the vegetables and bouquet garni, bring back to the boil, then reduce the heat and simmer with the lid on for about 5 hours. Season with salt and peppercorns.

Strain the stock and leave to cool. When cold, refrigerate for several hours. Skim off any fat that may form on the top and use stock as required.
Makes about 1.5 litres

CHICKEN STOCK
Fond blanc de volaille

1–2 chicken carcasses and bones
250 g chicken giblets, excluding the liver
2 litres cold water
2 onions, chopped
2 carrots, chopped
1 bouquet garni
1 teaspoon salt
freshly ground black pepper

Wash chicken carcasses, bones and giblets. Put them in a large straight-sided saucepan, add water and bring to the boil, removing any foam or fat that rises to the surface.

Add the chopped vegetables and bring back to the boil, then reduce the heat and simmer, covered, for about 3 hours. Add seasonings to taste.

Strain the stock then leave to cool. When cold, refrigerate for several hours. Skim off any fat that forms on the surface and use stock as required.
Makes about 1.5 litres

FISH STOCK
Fond de poisson

Fish stock will keep in the refrigerator for 3 days. If preferred, stock can be frozen. Freeze either in ice-cube trays or 1 cup quantities.

heads, bones and trimmings of a firm-
*   fleshed fish (snapper, whiting etc.)*
1 onion, finely chopped
½ cup white wine
4 parsley stalks, roughly chopped
5 black peppercorns
juice of ½ lemon
few celery leaves
1.5 litres water

Place all ingredients in a saucepan and add water to cover. Bring to the boil, reduce heat and simmer, for 20 minutes only. Skim occasionally. Strain and use as required.
Makes about 1.25 litres

COURT BOUILLON

1 litre cold water
1 teaspoon salt
1 small carrot, sliced
1 bay leaf
3 parsley stalks
¼ cup white wine or *vinegar*
60 g onion, sliced
sprig thyme
few celery leaves

Combine all ingredients in a large saucepan and bring slowly to the boil. Reduce the heat and simmer, covered, for 30 minutes. Strain before using.
Makes about 1 litre

Court Bouillon

Sauces

The French sauces fall into well-defined families. As we all know, every family is made up of quite unique components. It is the same with sauces. A pinch of this and a dash of that can transform the sauce base or 'mother' sauce, into a separate identity.

The following list gives the base sauces from which many delicious variations can be created.

White Sauces • Sauces Blanches
Brown Sauces • Sauces Brunes
Tomato Sauces • Sauces Tomates
The Hollandaise Family
The Mayonnaise Family
Oil and Vinegar Sauces • Vinaigrettes
Hot Butter Sauces • Sauces au Beurre
Cold Flavoured Butters • Beurres
Composés

White Sauces

There are two white sauces in French cooking which provide the basis for many delicious variations simply with the addition of butter, cream, herbs or wine. Both start with a roux — the flour and butter combination that thickens the sauce and which is slowly cooked before any liquid is added. Béchamel Sauce is a basic white sauce made with milk; white stock is added to the roux to make a Velouté Sauce.

BÉCHAMEL SAUCE

15 g butter
1 tablespoon flour
1 cup milk
salt and white pepper

Melt butter, add flour and cook, stirring constantly over a moderate heat for 1 minute. Off the heat gradually whisk in milk. Season and simmer for 3 minutes, stirring constantly.
Note: Béchamel Sauce can be made in advance. Place a piece of buttered greaseproof (waxproof) paper on the surface of sauce while storing or when keeping warm to prevent a skin from forming. Reheat sauce slowly, whisking constantly. Should any lumps form, pass sauce through a sieve.
Makes 1 cup

Variation:
For a thick Béchamel use 30 g butter and 2 tablespoons flour.

VELOUTÉ SAUCE

30 g butter
1 tablespoon flour
1 cup white stock (fish, veal or mutton see recipe)

Melt the butter in a medium-sized saucepan and when it starts to foam, add the flour, stirring vigorously with a wooden spoon over a low heat for 1 minute. Remove the saucepan from the heat and add the stock a little at a time, stirring constantly.

If the sauce begins turning lumpy, beat hard until the lumps have dissolved. Continue to add the stock until all has been used.

Return to the heat and stir as the sauce thickens and starts to boil. Boil for 3 minutes.
Makes 1 cup

CREAM SAUCE
Sauce crème
Sauce suprême

By adding cream, a Velouté Sauce becomes a Sauce Suprême and a Béchamel Sauce becomes Sauce Crème.

2 cups thick Béchamel or Velouté Sauce (see recipe)
salt and pepper, to taste
⅔ cup thickened (double) cream
2 teaspoons lemon juice

Heat the sauce until simmering. Gradually add the cream, beating well until the sauce reaches the desired consistency. Season and add lemon juice to taste.
Makes 2 cups

MORNAY SAUCE

This cheese sauce is delicious served with eggs, fish, poultry, pasta and vegetables.

1 cup Velouté or Béchamel Sauce (see recipe)
3 tablespoons grated Gruyère cheese
pinch grated nutmeg

Heat sauce until it is just boiling. Add the cheese and keep stirring until the cheese has melted.
Makes 1 cup

Variation:
Add 1 teaspoon of French mustard to make a tangier Mornay Sauce.

NANTUA SAUCE

When serving shellfish, keep a few of the shells, freeze them and use as required for adding colour to recipes such as the following sauce.

1½ cups Béchamel Sauce (see recipe)
½ cup Fish Stock (see recipe)
100 g cooked shells from lobster, crayfish or prawns (shrimps)
100 g butter
1 teaspoon brandy
pinch cayenne pepper

Place sauce in a pan adding the fish stock and stirring until smooth. Place over a medium heat and cook, stirring constantly until reduced by half.

Pound the crayfish or prawn shells using a mortar and pestle or a rolling pin to form fine particles the size of breadcrumbs. Leave the shells in the mortar and pestle or add to a mixing bowl and beat in the butter. When a bright orange colour has been achieved, rub the butter through a fine sieve to remove shell.

Add butter, brandy and cayenne pepper to the sauce and reheat. Serve with seafood or eggs.
Makes 1 cup

WHITE WINE AND SHALLOT SAUCE
Sauce Bercy

2 teaspoons finely chopped shallots (spring onions, scallions),
250 mL dry white wine
150 mL strong fish stock
2½ cups Velouté Sauce made with Fish Stock (see recipe)
100 g unsalted butter
freshly ground pepper
pinch finely chopped parsley

Melt a little of the butter in a small saucepan. Add the shallots and cook over a low heat for 5 minutes without browning. Add the wine and fish stock and simmer until reduced by ⅓. Remove from heat and beat in the Velouté Sauce.

Return to the heat and boil for 10 minutes. Remove and gradually add the remaining butter, beating until smooth. Season to taste and stir through the parsley. Serve with seafood.
Makes 3½ cups

White Wine and Shallot Sauce

FISH SAUCE
Sauce Normande

100 g mushrooms, finely chopped
1¼ cups fish stock
2½ cups Velouté Sauce, made with Fish
  Stock (see recipe)
150 mL liquid in which 4 oysters have
  been poached
4 egg yolks
3 tablespoons thickened (double) cream
100 g unsalted butter

Simmer the mushrooms in the fish stock for 3 minutes then combine with the Velouté Sauce and oyster liquid. Simmer over a medium heat until reduced by ⅓.

Beat together the egg yolks and cream. Add a little of the hot sauce then return to the saucepan and cook over a low heat until thickened.

Remove from heat and gradually beat in the butter.
Makes 4 cups

Cream Sauce (see recipe page 12)

Brown Sauces

RICH BROWN SAUCE
Sauce Espagnole

This sauce is dark reddish-brown in colour and is the result of vegetables and stock being simmered together and reduced to create the basis for many sauce recipes.

50 g dripping
50 g streaky bacon, finely chopped
1 small onion, finely chopped
1 stalk celery, finely chopped
½ cup flour
2 cups beef stock
70 g mushrooms, wiped and finely chopped
2–3 stems parsley
2 tablespoons tomato paste
2 tablespoons Madeira or sherry
salt and pepper to taste

Melt butter in a heavy-based saucepan. Add the bacon, onion and celery and cook for 5 minutes or until the vegetables are a nutty brown colour. Stir in the flour and continue to cook, very gently, stirring occasionally until the flour is a golden brown colour. The browning of the flour contributes to the colour of the sauce but do not allow it to burn or the flavour will be ruined.

Gradually stir in most of the stock and slowly bring the sauce to the boil, stirring constantly. Add the remaining stock and mushrooms, reduce the heat and simmer, covered, for 30 minutes. Add the remaining ingredients, re-cover and simmer a further 15 minutes.

Strain the sauce through a sieve pressing the vegetables to extract as much sauce as possible. Reheat the sauce, taste and adjust the seasoning as required.
Makes 2 cups

DEMI-GLACE SAUCE

1 cup Rich Brown Sauce (see recipe)
1 cup Brown Beef Stock (see recipe)
¼ cup Madeira

Combine sauce and stock, bring to the boil and simmer until reduced to approximately 1⅓ cups. Add Madeira, strain through a sieve. Taste to adjust seasoning then serve.
Makes about 1⅔ cups

BORDELAISE SAUCE

2 shin bones, halved
200 mL red wine
1 shallot (spring onion, scallion) bulb end
* only, finely chopped*
sprig of fresh thyme
1 small bay leaf
1 cup Demi-glace Sauce (see recipe)
20 g butter
1 tablespoon finely chopped parsley

Place the shin bones in a large pan and cover with cold water. Place over a low heat and simmer very gently until the marrow comes away from the bone. Remove from the heat and lift the marrow from the bone. Chop and measure the marrow. You will need 60 g so reserve the remaining marrow for another recipe. Place the wine in a saucepan with the shallot, thyme and bay leaf.

Bring to the boil and cook until reduced to ⅓ cup. Strain the wine and return to the saucepan with Demi-glace Sauce. Simmer until reduced to 1 cup. Add the butter and strain the sauce.

Just before serving, add the marrow and chopped parsley but do not stir into the sauce.

Serve with grilled steak or other grilled meat.

Makes 1 cup

Rich Brown Sauce

TOMATO AND MUSHROOM SAUCE
Sauce chasseur

¼ cup finely chopped shallots (spring
* onions, scallions)*
375 g ripe tomatoes, cored, peeled and
* seeded*
1 small clove garlic, crushed
salt and pepper
½ teaspoon finely chopped fresh basil or ¼
* teaspoon dried basil*
½ cup white wine
1 cup Rich Brown Sauce (see recipe)
30 g butter
250 g button mushrooms, finely chopped

Cook the shallots in a frying pan over a low heat for 1 minute. Add the tomatoes, garlic, seasonings and herbs. Cover and simmer for 5 minutes. Add the wine and sauce stirring until blended. Boil rapidly for 5 minutes or until the sauce has thickened slightly.

Melt the butter in a separate frying pan. Add the mushrooms and cook for 4 minutes or until tender. Add the mushrooms to the sauce and simmer for 2 minutes.

Serve with steak or veal escallops.

Makes 1½ cups

DEVILLED SAUCE
Sauce diable

50 g shallots (spring onions, scallions),
* finely chopped*
⅔ cup dry white wine
1 tablespoon wine vinegar
6 white peppercorns, crushed
1 dried chilli
2½ cups Demi-glace or Rich Brown Sauce
* (see recipes)*
salt and pepper

Boil the shallots in a saucepan with the wine, vinegar, peppercorns and chilli until reduced by ½.

Stir in the Demi-glace or Rich Brown Sauce and simmer for 15 minutes. Season with salt and pepper, then strain through a fine sieve.

Serve with grilled chicken legs, grilled gammon steaks or fish.

Makes about 2½ cups

HERB SAUCE
Sauce aux fine herbes

½ cup white wine
2 sprigs parsley, finely chopped
1 sprig thyme, stalk removed and leaves
* finely chopped*
2 teaspoons chopped chervil
2 teaspoons chopped tarragon
1¼ cups Rich Brown Sauce (see recipe)

Place the wine in a small saucepan until reduced by half. Add the herbs and let stand for 10 minutes.

Add the sauce and simmer for 2 minutes then serve.

Makes 1½ cups

15

Herbed Tomato Sauce

TARRAGON SAUCE
Sauce à l'estragon

½ cup dry white wine
sprig tarragon
1 ¼ cups Demi-glace or Rich Brown Sauce
(see recipes)
50 g butter
1 teaspoon chopped tarragon leaves

Place the wine in a small saucepan and simmer until reduced by half. Add the tarragon sprig and let stand for 10 minutes. Then add the Demi-glace or Rich Brown Sauce. Reduce the sauce by ½, strain through a very fine sieve, then away from the heat, add the butter.

Season with 1 teaspoon chopped tarragon leaves.
Makes 1½ cups

HERBED TOMATO SAUCE
Sauce Italienne

¼ cup olive oil
1 onion, finely chopped
2 cloves garlic, crushed (minced)
1 small red capsicum (pepper), finely chopped
1 kg ripe tomatoes, peeled, seeded and finely chopped
3 bay leaves
2 ½ teaspoons sugar
2 teaspoons finely chopped basil or 1 teaspoon dried basil
2 teaspoons finely chopped oregano or 1 teaspoon dried oregano
½ cup dry white wine

Heat oil and sauté onion for 5 minutes. Add garlic and capsicum and sauté a further 2 minutes. Add remaining ingredients and simmer, stirring occasionally for 1 hour or until thickened.
Note: Herbed Tomato Sauce will keep up to 5 days refrigerated or may be frozen.
Makes approximately 2¾ cups

16

Egg Yolk and Butter Sauces

The Hollandaise Family

Hollandaise with whipped cream Sauce Chantilly

Fold 100 mL whipped cream into each cup of Hollandaise, just before serving.

Orange flavoured Hollandaise Sauce Maltaise

Fold the grated rind of 1 orange and 2–3 tablespoons orange juice through 1 cup Hollandaise.

Hollandaise Sauce

HOLLANDAISE SAUCE

3 tablespoons white wine vinegar
5 black peppercorns
½ bay leaf
3 egg yolks
180–250 g unsalted butter cut into cubes and slightly softened
salt and white pepper to taste
squeeze lemon juice
fresh dill, to garnish

Simmer vinegar, peppercorns and bay leaf together in a small saucepan until the mixture reduces to 3 teaspoons. Strain and set aside.

Place the egg yolks and 1 tablespoon of butter together in a heatproof bowl and whisk together, adding the flavoured vinegar. Place the bowl over a saucepan of gently simmering water making sure the bowl does not touch the water.

Whisk the sauce constantly, adding the butter a little at a time. If the butter is added too quickly, the sauce may curdle. You may not need all the butter but the finished sauce should be a light, creamy colour, of foamy consistency and thick enough to coat the back of a metal spoon. Use immediately over meat or seafood dishes.
Makes 1½–2 cups

Variations:

Hollandaise with capers

Add 1 tablespoon capers to each cup of Hollandaise.

Hollandaise with beaten egg whites
Hollandaise avec blancs d'oeufs

Fold 2 stiffly beaten egg whites into 1 cup Hollandaise. This lightens the sauce.

The Béarnaise Family

BÉARNAISE SAUCE

Béarnaise Sauce is an excellent accompaniment to grilled or baked rich fish such as tuna, Spanish mackerel, eel or salmon.

This sauce has the same keeping qualities as Hollandaise Sauce.

180 g butter
3 tablespoons vinegar
3 tablespoons dry white wine
8 black peppercorns, crushed (minced)
salt
2 tablespoons finely chopped shallots
  (spring onions, scallions)
1½ tablespoons finely chopped tarragon
3 egg yolks

Melt butter, remove foam from the surface and cool to tepid.

Combine vinegar, wine, peppercorns, salt, shallots and 1 tablespoon tarragon. Boil until reduced to 2 tablespoons. Strain and cool to room temperature. Add to egg yolks and whisk for 1 minute.

Place the mixture in a double boiler over hot water and beat vigorously until thick and creamy. The base of the pan containing mixture should never be more than hand hot. Remove from heat and whisk in tepid butter, add a few drops at a time, until sauce starts to thicken, and thereafter in a very thin stream. Do not add sediment at the bottom of butter.

Stir in remaining chopped tarragon.
Makes approximately 1 cup

Variations:

Béarnaise with green peppercorns
Béarnaise au poivre vert

Omit tarragon added at the end of the sauce and replace it with 1 tablespoon drained, crushed green peppercorns for each cup of sauce.

Béarnaise with tomato purée
Sauce Choron

Add 1½ tablespoons tomato purée to each cup of sauce.

EASY BÉARNAISE SAUCE

1 cup Béchamel Sauce (see recipe)
2 tablespoons wine vinegar
2 tablespoons dry white wine
1 teaspoon dried tarragon
2 teaspoons chopped white of shallot (spring onion, scallion)
pinch salt
pinch white pepper
pinch fresh or dried herbs
2 egg yolks, lightly beaten
2 tablespoons soft butter

Prepare Béchamel Sauce then set it aside with a covering of greaseproof (waxproof) paper.

Simmer vinegar and wine with herbs, shallot and seasonings until the liquid is reduced by ½ then strain. Pour Béchamel over egg yolks, whisk, then add butter and reduced liquid. Beat thoroughly and serve immediately.
Makes 1½ cups

Béarnaise Sauce

Oil and Vinegar Sauces

The Mayonnaise Family

MAYONNAISE
Sauce mayonnaise

A very popular cold sauce with many exciting variations, two classics being Green Sauce and Tartare Sauce. Mayonnaise blends particularly well with the flavours of chicken, seafood and eggs.

4 egg yolks
salt and freshly ground black pepper
1 teaspoon prepared mustard
250 mL vegetable oil
1–2 tablespoons white wine vinegar

Whisk egg yolks, salt, pepper and mustard together until thick, then gradually add the oil, drop by drop, whisking constantly until ¼ cup has been incorporated. Add the rest of the oil in a thin steady stream and continue to whisk. Check the consistency occasionally and when the mayonnaise begins to thicken and whisking is difficult, add a little vinegar to thin down the sauce.

When all the oil is incorporated, taste and adjust the seasoning with salt, pepper and vinegar.
Makes 1 cup

GREEN SAUCE
Sauce verte

60 g spinach leaf, rinsed and chopped
2 teaspoons chopped tarragon
2 teaspoons chopped chervil
2 tablespoons chopped chives or watercress
1 cup Mayonnaise (see recipe)

Blanch the spinach and herbs then refresh in cold water. Squeeze dry with a clean tea towel before adding to the Mayonnaise and blending well. Serve over pasta or seafood or as a dipping sauce for prawns.
Makes 2½ cups

RÉMOULADE SAUCE

1 quantity of Tartare Sauce (see recipe)
anchovy paste to taste

Combine all ingredients, using a small quantity only of anchovy paste e.g. ½ teaspoon should be sufficient.
Makes 1½ cups

Mayonnaise

TARTARE SAUCE

1 cup Mayonnaise (see recipe)
60 g gherkin, finely diced
30 g capers, chopped
parsley, finely chopped

Combine all the ingredients in a bowl and mix together until they have a smooth consistency. Tartare Sauce can be served as an accompaniment to most seafood dishes whether hot or cold.

Store in well-sealed jar, preferably glass, in the refrigerator for up to 10 days if home-made Mayonnaise was used, or for about one month otherwise.
Makes 1½ cups

MAYONNAISE WITH CREAM
Sauce chantilly

1 cup Mayonnaise (see recipe)
½ cup whipped cream
squeeze lemon juice

Combine all ingredients and mix together until smooth.
Makes 1½ cups

VINAIGRE VIEUX
de vin rouge
7°
vieilli en foudres de chêne
selon les anciennes
traditions

BORNIER DIJON

toutes mes bouteilles doivent
porter le cachet de ma maison

1 L.

OIL AND VINEGAR DRESSING
Sauce vinaigrette

¼ cup white wine vinegar
pinch salt
pinch dry mustard powder
½ cup salad oil
freshly ground black pepper
2 tablespoons parsley or a combination of parsley and tarragon, finely chopped

Beat the vinegar in a bowl with the salt and mustard powder. Gradually add the oil drop by drop and season with pepper. Stir in the optional herbs and pour the dressing over the salad just before serving.
Makes ¾ cup

MUSTARD SAUCE
Sauce moutarde

2 tablespoons prepared French mustard
3 tablespoons boiling water
¼–½ cup olive oil or salad oil
salt and pepper
1 tablespoon lemon juice
1–2 tablespoons chopped parsley or green herbs

Warm a small mixing bowl by rinsing in hot water. Add the mustard and beat with a wire whisk adding the water drop by drop. Beat in the olive oil drop by drop to make a thick, creamy sauce.

Add the salt, pepper and lemon juice to taste. Stir in the herbs. Store sauce in a screw-topped jar in the refrigerator.
Makes 1 cup.

RAVIGOTE SAUCE

1¼ cups Oil and Vinegar Dressing (see recipe)
1 teaspoon capers, chopped
1 teaspoon very finely chopped shallots (spring onions, scallions)
1 tablespoon chopped green herbs (parsley, chives, tarragon)

Combine all ingredients in a screw-topped jar. Shake until well-combined then use as required for hot or cold boiled beef, chicken or seafood.
Makes 1½ cups

Oil and Vinegar Sauces

Other Useful Sauces

CRÈME FRAÎCHE

Popular with nouvelle cuisine chefs, Crème Fraîche is a light cream with a slight tang.

¾ cup cream
1 tablespoon yoghurt

Stir cream and yoghurt together in a jar, keep covered overnight or for 8 hours in a warm place. Alternatively, place loosely covered jar in microwave oven and cook on lowest temperature (50°C) for 4 minutes.

Before using, chill cream well. It will thicken as it chills.
Makes about 1 cup

Left to right: Parsley Butter, Orange Butter and Mustard Butter

CREAM DRESSING
Vinaigrette à la crème

½ small white onion, finely chopped
salt and pepper
juice 1 lemon
3 tablespoons cream

Combine the onion, salt, pepper and lemon juice in a salad bowl. Gradually stir in the cream.
Makes ⅔ cup

WHITE BUTTER SAUCE

This sauce is the classic Beurre Blanc with white wine added. For a more traditional sauce simply leave out the wine.

3 tablespoons white wine vinegar
3 tablespoons dry white wine
2 tablespoons finely chopped shallots (spring onions, scallions)
250 g butter, chilled and cut into small pieces
salt and white pepper

Boil vinegar, wine and shallots until reduced to 1 tablespoon. Gradually whisk in butter over a very low heat. The sauce should be smooth and creamy, butter should soften, not actually melt. Season to taste.
Note: The first stage of the sauce can be made in advance. However, butter should be added just before serving. Thereafter, the completed sauce will keep only a few minutes over warm water.
Makes 1 cup

Flavoured Butters and Compound Butters

Beurres Composés

Flavoured butters are easily prepared, can be made in advance, freeze well and have a variety of uses in seafood cookery. Use them to baste while baking or grilling, as an enrichment to sauces or soups, as a spread for hors d'oeuvre or place a piece of flavoured butter on top of grilled seafood just as it is sent to the table.

MUSTARD BUTTER
Beurre de moutarde

125 g butter, softened
1–2 tablespoons Dijon-style mustard
salt

Cream together all ingredients and use as desired.

PARSLEY BUTTER
Beurre maître d'hotel

125 g butter, softened
juice ½ lemon
2 tablespoons finely chopped parsley
salt and ground black pepper

Cream together all ingredients and use as desired.

Variations:

Garlic Butter
Beurre à l'ail

Omit the parsley and substitute 4 cloves garlic, crushed or to taste. Serve with prawns.

Capsicum (green pepper) butter
Beurre au poivron

Omit the parsley and substitute ½ capsicum, very finely chopped.

Orange butter
Beurre à l'orange

Omit the parsley and substitute the rind of 1 orange, finely grated.

Clarified butter
Beurre clarifié

Heat required quantity of unsalted butter in a pan until hot. Remove from heat and allow to stand until milk solids settle to base of pan. Carefully pour clarified butter into another container, leaving milk solids behind.

SOUP OF THE DAY
Soupe du Jour

BEEF CONSOMMÉ
Consommé

2 litres chilled Brown Beef Stock (see recipe)
1 carrot, peeled and chopped
1 leek (green part only), chopped
2 stalks celery, chopped
2 egg whites
1.5 kg very lean beef, minced
few sprigs chopped chervil and tarragon or 1 bouquet garni
⅔ cup cold water
peppercorns
1 tablespoon sherry (optional)

Remove all fat from surface of Brown Beef Stock and place in a large pan.

Mix vegetables with egg whites in a large bowl and stir in beef, herbs and water. Add vegetable mixture to stock, mix together, then bring slowly to the boil, stirring to the bottom of pan to prevent mixture from sticking. Keep whisking mixture until a thick froth starts to form and set on the surface. As soon as mixture starts to boil, turn down heat and simmer, covered, for about 1½ hours without stirring. From time to time remove any fat which rises to the surface (there should be hardly any at all).

At the end of the cooking time, pour contents of pan through double muslin over a sieve, on which the peppercorns have been put, into a bowl underneath. At first hold back the egg white crust with a spoon, then let it slip onto the cloth. Pour soup through again and over the egg white filter. The consommé should now be completely clear. Reheat, check seasoning and add sherry, if liked, to improve flavour.
Serves 8

Variations:

Consommé julienne

Add cooked matchstick-thin strips of vegetables (carrot, turnip, celery) to the hot soup.

Consommé à la madrilène

Add chopped tomatoes and celery to soup and serve cold.

Consommé au riz

Add a small quantity of cooked long-grain rice to the hot soup.

Quick consommé

Heat canned consommé gently in a pan and stir in 1 tablespoon sherry or Madeira (or to taste) to boost the flavour. Garnish and serve as for home-made consommé.

CHICKEN CONSOMMÉ VERMICELLI
Consommé de volaille aux vermicelli

350 g lean beef, minced
pinch salt
1 egg white and shell
1.8 litres cold Chicken Stock (see recipe)
175 g chopped mixed vegetables (onion, carrot, celery, leek)
bouquet garni
3–4 peppercorns
2 chicken legs, skinned
⅓ cup vermicelli

Thoroughly mix together beef, salt, egg white, shell and 1¼ cups of cold Chicken Stock in a heavy-based saucepan. Add chopped vegetables, the rest of the stock, bouquet garni, peppercorns and chicken legs and bring slowly to the boil over a gentle heat, stirring occasionally. Allow to boil rapidly for 5–10 seconds, then reduce heat. Leave to simmer very gently for 1½–2 hours without stirring. Do not let liquid reach boiling point, as the foam layer will break up and cloud the consommé.

Meanwhile, cook vermicelli in boiling salted water for 5 minutes and drain.

When soup is cooked, lift out chicken legs, strain soup through double muslin and remove all fat from the surface with absorbent kitchen paper (paper towels). Adjust seasoning to taste. Remove bones from chicken legs and dice the meat. Add vermicelli, allow it to warm through, and serve.
Note: To enrich vermicelli, cook it in a

little of the strained soup rather than salted water. For economy, chicken legs can be replaced by 2 chicken stock cubes (instant chicken bouillon granules).
Serves 6

ONION SOUP
Soupe à l'oignon

60 g butter
3 large onions, thinly sliced
1 tablespoon flour
½ teaspoon salt
freshly ground black pepper
5 cups Brown Beef Stock (see recipe)
4 Cheese Croûtes (see recipe)

In a heavy-based saucepan, melt the butter, add the sliced onions and cook slowly stirring occasionally, until golden brown and tender. Sprinkle on the flour and stir for a few minutes to cook the flour. Season with salt and pepper. Gradually add the stock, stirring constantly. Bring to a boil, lower the heat and let the soup simmer, partially covered, for 30 minutes.

Place the Cheese Croûtes in the base of individual soup dishes. Pour the soup over the croûtes and serve immediately.
Serves 4

Onion Soup

FARMHOUSE SOUP
Potage fermière

50 g butter
2 carrots, peeled and diced
2 turnips, peeled and diced
white portion of 2 leeks, sliced
2 stalks celery, sliced
500 g bacon joint, rind removed
2 litres White or Chicken Stock (see recipe)
½ green cabbage, sliced thinly
salt and pepper
150 g French beans, stringed
2 potatoes, peeled and diced very small
150 g peas, shelled
¾ cup Gruyère cheese, grated and croûtons, to serve

Melt butter in a large pan. Add carrots, turnips, leeks and celery and soften on low heat for 10 minutes, stirring occasionally.

Wash bacon in cold water then place in a saucepan and cover with cold water. Bring to the boil and simmer for 10 minutes on a low heat. Drain and rinse in cold water.

Add stock to vegetables, then add bacon, cabbage and salt and pepper. Bring to the boil, then reduce heat, cover and simmer very gently for about 1¼ hours.

Cut beans into pieces abut 4 cm in length. Cover potatoes with water and leave to soak.

About 20 minutes before the end of cooking time, drain potatoes and add them to soup with peas and green beans. Leave to finish cooking.

Heat a soup tureen. Put grated Gruyère cheese into a bowl. Remove bacon, cut into cubes and put into tureen. Add soup and serve with croûtons. Serve Gruyère cheese separately.
Serves 4

CREAM OF CARROT SOUP
Crème de Crecy

20 g butter or margarine
2 medium onions, chopped
1 kg carrots, chopped
salt and pepper
2 litres White Stock (see recipe)
2 tablespoons rice
2 medium potatoes, chopped
1 egg yolk
¼ cup thickened (double) cream

Farmhouse Soup

Heat half the butter in a large saucepan, add onions and fry without colouring, over low heat until soft and translucent. Stir carrots into the pan and add stock and salt to taste. Cover and simmer over moderate heat for 30 minutes.

Wash rice under cold running water. Add rice with potatoes to pan and cook for further 30 minutes. Purée in food processor or blender or work through a sieve.

Blend egg yolk with cream in a bowl. Season generously with salt and pepper and beat again. Stir in a little hot soup; then return egg yolk mixture to soup. Reheat gently but do not boil. Serve hot.
Serves 6

VICHYSSOISE

60 g butter
4 leeks, well-washed and white part chopped
1 onion, chopped
1 litre Chicken Stock (see recipe)
1 tablespoon parsley, chopped
1 stalk celery, chopped
3 potatoes, peeled and sliced thinly
salt and pepper to taste
1¼ cups milk
1¼ cups cream
whipped cream and fine leek needle threads, to garnish

Melt butter in a saucepan and sauté white part of leek and onion gently until tender but not brown. Add Chicken Stock, parsley, celery and potatoes, salt and pepper and simmer for 15 minutes. Cool slightly then purée in blender or food processor or pour through a sieve. Test for flavour, adding salt and pepper if required. Reheat gently with milk and cream. Chill thoroughly and serve in chilled bowls with 1 spoonful whipped cream floating on top and a sprinkle of finely shredded leek needles prepared from light green tops which have been dropped in iced water and drained.
Serves 6

CHILLED WATERCRESS AND POTATO SOUP
Crème de cressonière

1 bunch watercress
20 g butter
1 onion, finely chopped
1 stalk celery, chopped

2 medium potatoes, peeled and cubed
3 cups Chicken Stock (see recipe)
1 tablespoon lemon juice
½ teaspoon salt
black pepper, ground
good ⅔ cup thickened (double) cream

Wash watercress and put some leaves aside for decoration. Chop remaining leaves and stems into small pieces.

Melt butter in a saucepan. Add onion and celery to pan and cook for 3 minutes.

Add potatoes, stock, chopped watercress, lemon juice, salt and pepper. Cover and simmer for 30 minutes. Remove from heat and cool a little and then pour through a sieve or purée in a blender and strain into a container with a lid. Taste and adjust seasoning if necessary. Cover and chill for 2 hours. Just before serving stir in cream and reserved watercress.
Serves 4

SOUP OF FROGS' LEGS AND WATERCRESS
Soupe de grenouilles au cresson

1 litre Fish Stock (see recipe)
24 frogs' legs
1 cup dry white wine
60 g shallots (spring onions, scallions), finely chopped
1 tablespoon finely chopped tarragon
salt and ground black pepper
1 bunch watercress
6 egg yolks
1 cup Crème Fraîche (see recipe) or cream

Bring Fish Stock to boil before adding frogs' legs, leaving to simmer 2–3 minutes. Bone frogs' legs and keep warm.

Place wine, shallots, tarragon, salt and pepper in saucepan and simmer until wine has almost all evaporated. Add this to Fish Stock.

Remove large stalks from watercress, reserving about 6 sprigs for garnish. Blanch remaining watercress in Fish Stock and purée.

Beat egg yolks and Crème Fraîche (or cream) together. Gradually whisk 1 cup hot Fish Stock into egg and cream mixtures and pour this mixture into remaining stock, whisking constantly over gentle heat until lightly thickened. Do not allow to boil. Add puréed watercress and heat through.

Arrange boned frogs' legs in 6 soup bowls, pour in hot soup and garnish with reserved watercress leaves.
Serves 6

FISH SOUP WITH FENNEL, ORANGE AND AIOLI
Bourride

1.5 kg assorted fish
1.5 litre water
2 onions, chopped
½ medium-sized bulb fennel, chopped
3 cloves garlic, crushed (minced)
1 teaspoon chopped thyme
1 teaspoon chopped parsley
2 bay leaves
zest 1 orange
salt and ground black pepper
16 Croûtes (see recipe)
1 cup Aioli (see recipe)
5 egg yolks

Fillet fish, removing all skin and bones and cut into 2 cm pieces. Reserve heads and bones.

Combine fish heads and bones with water, onions, fennel, garlic, thyme, parsley, bay leaves, orange zest, salt and pepper. Simmer 20 minutes. Strain through 2 layers damp muslin, pressing hard against bones.

Reheat liquid. Add fish pieces and simmer 3 minutes or until fish flakes easily when tested. Transfer the fish pieces to a soup tureen and keep warm.

Whisk Aioli with egg yolks. Gradually whisk in 2 cups of hot fish liquid. Cook over a very gentle heat, whisking continuously until soup thickens slightly. Do not boil. Pour soup over fish pieces and garnish with Croûtes.

Serves 6

Fish Soup with Fennel, Orange and Aioli

FISH SOUP
Bouillabaise

1 litre Fish Stock (see recipe)
½ cup white wine
250 g tomatoes, peeled, seeded and sliced
1 clove garlic, chopped
2 strips orange rind
2 sprigs parsley and *fennel*
sprig thyme
pinch saffron threads

ROUILLE

1 green capsicum (pepper)
1 fresh chilli
2–3 cloves garlic
250 g can pimiento
1½ tablespoons olive oil
breadcrumbs
salt and pepper

FISH
750 g fish fillets
250 g green prawns (shrimps), shelled and deveined
375 g mussels, cleaned
4 green king prawns, to garnish

Place stock, wine, tomatoes, garlic, orange rind, herbs and saffron in a pan. Bring to boil, reduce heat and simmer for 20 minutes, then strain.

Seed and halve capsicum and chilli and place in a pan. Cover with cold water, bring to boil and simmer for 3 minutes. Drain well and refresh under cold running water.

Using a mortar and pestle, crush garlic and pimiento. Add blanched capsicum and chilli and when smooth gradually add oil. Add enough breadcrumbs to form a firm mixture. Taste and adjust seasoning.

Bring cooked liquid to boil. Cut fish in strips about 3 cm wide and add to pan. Simmer for 2 minutes. Add prawns and mussels and simmer until fish, prawns and mussels are cooked, about 5 minutes. Discard any mussels that remain closed.

Fry king prawns in a little oil until colour changes and use these to garnish the soup.

Serve soup hot, topped with a spoonful of rouille and with crusty bread.

Serves 4

CREAMY MUSSEL SOUP
Soupe de moules

1 kg white fish fillets (whiting, snapper, etc.)
1 cup dry white wine
60 g shallots (spring onions, scallions), finely chopped
1.5 kg mussels, cleaned, beards removed
45 g butter
2 onions, chopped
3 cloves garlic, crushed (minced)
2 leeks, well-washed and chopped
2 cup Fish Stock (see recipe)
750 g ripe tomatoes, peeled and chopped
½ bulb fennel, chopped
2 bay leaves
1 tablespoon chopped thyme
large pinch saffron threads or powder
ground black pepper
1 cup Crème Fraîche (see recipe) or cream

Cut fish into 2 cm pieces.

Bring wine and shallots to the boil. Simmer 5 minutes. Add mussels, cover and simmer a further 5 minutes, shaking pan occasionally to ensure even heat distribution. Discard any mussels which remain closed. Remove mussels from their shells and keep warm. Strain cooking liquid through 2 layers damp muslin.

Fish Soup

CROÛTONS

These keep well in the freezer. Store in an airtight container and reheat in the oven before serving.

½ 'day-old' loaf bread
oil for deep-frying

Remove the crust and cut the bread into 1 cm cubes.

Heat the oil for deep-frying in a straight-sided pan. Add the bread cubes a few at a time until golden brown. Remove from the oil using a slotted spoon and drain on absorbent paper (paper towels). Repeat with remaining bread.

Serve separately as a garnish for soup.
Serves 4–6

Sauté onions, garlic and leeks in butter for 3 minutes. Add strained reserved liquid, Fish Stock, tomatoes, fennel, bay leaves, thyme, saffron and pepper. Simmer 30 minutes. Pass the mixture through a fine sieve, pressing hard to extract as much vegetable purée as possible.

Reheat the mixture, add the fish pieces and simmer 5 minutes or until the fish flakes easily when tested. Add the mussels and Crème Fraîche or cream. Heat through but do not boil.
Serves 6

PRAWN BISQUE
Bisque de crevettes

50 g butter
¼ cup flour
1 litre milk
salt and pepper
225 g unshelled prawns (shrimps)
2 tablespoons oil
1 shallot (spring onion, scallion), chopped
1 small onion, chopped
1 stalk celery, chopped
1 small bouquet garni
¼ cup brandy
5 tomatoes, peeled, seeded, chopped
½ cup dry white wine

50 g peeled prawns, fresh or frozen
½ cup thickened (double) cream

Melt butter in a double saucepan and blend in flour to make a roux. Cook for about 1 minute without letting it colour. Then, using a wooden spoon gradually blend in milk off the heat and return to stove, bringing to the boil. Season with salt and pepper and cook for 20 minutes over a low heat, stirring occasionally.

Shell the prawns and place shells into a muslin bag. Heat oil in a pan. When hot add prawns, vegetables (but not the tomatoes) and bouquet garni. Cook gently for about 5 minutes or until vegetables are soft.

Pour in brandy, heat for about 1 minute, then set alight. When flames die down, add tomatoes and white wine and muslin bag. Add salt and season liberally with pepper, then cook for 20 minutes.

Remove prawns from pan. Chop them and return to pan. Add the white sauce, mix and cook slowly for another 15 minutes.

Pour soup through a fine strainer, pressing down well with a wooden spoon, back into pan. Bring to the boil again, check seasoning and add peeled prawns.

Pour cream into heated tureen, add soup, while stirring vigorously, and serve.
Serves 4

CROÛTES

Bread toasts are served with soup and provide body to the recipe. Toasting maintains the bread's character and prevents it from becoming a soggy mess when added to the soup.

12–16 slices French bread, cut
* 1.5–2.5 cm thick*
¼ cup olive oil
1 clove garlic, cut in half

Arrange the bread in a single layer on a baking tray and place in a preheated oven at 180°C (350°F) for 30 minutes or until the bread is dried out and golden brown. Half-way through baking, baste the bread with olive oil. After baking rub each piece with the garlic.
Serves 4–6

CHEESE CROÛTES
Croûtes au fromage

1 quantity Toasted French Bread (see recipe)
1 cup grated Swiss or Parmesan cheese
¼ cup olive oil

Sprinkle the cheese over one side of the croûtes and drizzle over drops of olive oil. Place under a preheated grill and cook until the cheese is golden brown and melted.
Serves 4–6

THE FIRST COURSE
Hors d'oeuvres

SALADE NIÇOISE

This famous salad from Nice is a meal in itself when served with French bread. It also makes a good accompaniment to a meal, such as fish stew that needs a vegetable and a salad. Omit the tuna when the salad accompanies fish or meat dishes. There are as many ways to make this salad as there are cooks in Nice!

1 bunch endive
1 cos lettuce
3 tomatoes, sliced
150 g French beans, lightly cooked
200 g pontiac or new potatoes, cooked and diced
3 hard-boiled eggs, sliced
1 onion, thinly sliced
1 green capsicum (pepper), thinly sliced
12 black olives
1 × 425 g can tuna, drained and flaked
½ cup chopped chervil or parsley

DRESSING
1 clove garlic
4 anchovy fillets, drained
ground black pepper
¼ teaspoon sugar
1 teaspoon finely chopped fresh basil or ½ teaspoon dried basil
2 tablespoons white wine vinegar
4 tablespoons olive oil

Line a large salad bowl with the endive and lettuce. Arrange all the other ingredients attractively on the lettuce. Prepare the dressing by pounding garlic in a mortar and pestle. Add anchovies, pepper, sugar and basil and continue to pound. Combine this mixture with the vinegar and olive oil. Pour over the salad.
Serves 4–6

HAM AND CHEESE BAKED MUSHROOMS
Champignons farcis

16 mushroom caps and stalks
FILLING
½ cup fresh white breadcrumbs
½ cup finely grated Parmesan cheese
250 g ham, chopped
2 tablespoons capers, finely chopped
½ cup grated Swiss cheese
1 clove garlic, crushed (minced)
salt and ground black pepper
lemon juice
2 tablespoons olive oil

GARNISH
8 slices smoked ham
6 lettuce leaves
1 tablespoons lemon juice

Carefully remove stalks from mushrooms. Chop stalks and mix them with filling ingredients except for seasoning, lemon juice and oil.

Arrange mushroom caps in a buttered ovenproof dish. Season with a sprinkle of salt and pepper and a squeeze of lemon juice. Spoon filling evenly into caps, shaping a little. Sprinkle with olive oil and bake for 8 minutes at 200°C (400°F).

Cut ham into circles with a scone cutter. Heat lettuce with lemon juice very gently in a covered saucepan until it has wilted.

Place a ham circle under each mushroom cap and serve on the bed of lettuce.
Serves 4–6

RICE AND TOMATO SALAD
Salade de riz aux tomates

1 cup long-grain rice
small piece lemon
salt and freshly ground black pepper
¼ cup olive oil
2 teaspoons tarragon vinegar
4 large tomatoes, skinned
1 tablespoon finely chopped chives

Wash rice with plenty of water. Bring 6 cups water to the boil adding a good pinch of salt and the lemon. Gradually add rice keeping water on the boil. Cook for 12 minutes or until rice is tender. Drain, remove lemon then season well with salt and pepper. Stir through oil and vinegar and allow to cool. Spoon into a serving dish.

Slice tomatoes and arrange over rice. Sprinkle with chopped chives.

Serve by itself or as an accompaniment to a main meal.
Serves 4

WARM GOAT CHEESE AND WALNUT SALAD
Salade tiède au fromage de chèvre et aux noix

DRESSING
1 tablespoon sherry vinegar
½ teaspoon dry mustard
salt and pepper to taste
pinch sugar
3 tablespoons safflower oil
1 tablespoon walnut oil

SALAD
⅓ cup walnuts, finely chopped
200 g goat cheese
curly endive
radicchio, washed, dried and torn into bite-sized pieces
2 shallots (spring onions, scallions), finely chopped
½ teaspoon chopped chervil

Prepare dressing by combining all ingredients and shaking in a glass jar until blended. Taste and adjust flavour if necessary.

Sprinkle nuts over cheese and press into surface. Place on a baking sheet and cook 3 minutes in oven at 200°C (400°F).

Combine salad greens. Toss with dressing in serving bowl.

Serve salad greens with warm cheese.
Serves 4

Salade Niçoise

Green Salad with Blue Cheese Dressing

GREEN SALAD WITH BLUE CHEESE DRESSING
Salade verte au bresse bleu

75 g blue-veined cheese
1 cup thickened (double) cream
pinch cayenne pepper
2 teaspoons finely chopped chives
2 heads soft lettuce

Blend together the cheese and cream until soft then push through a sieve to remove any lumps. Season with pepper and gently stir in the chives.

Wash the lettuce, remove the cores and separate into leaves. Place in a salad bowl and pour over the cheese dressing.

Serve immediately.
Serves 6

POACHED OYSTERS WITH WATERCRESS SAUCE
Huitres à la cresson

24 oysters, in the half shell
1–2 lemons
1 bunch watercress
1 bouquet garni
1 tablespoon onion, finely chopped
1 tablespoon carrot, finely chopped
½ cup dry white wine
1 cup water
½ cup cream

Remove oysters from shell and place in a bowl with their liquid.

Carefully peel rind of lemons, making sure no pith is included. Cut lemon rind into julienne strips (matchsticks) and blanch in boiling water for 3 minutes. Drain, refresh in running water and set aside.

Pick leaves from watercress and wash well, then blanch in boiling water for 4 minutes. Drain well and purée in a blender or food processor. Measure ⅔ cup of purée and dilute with cream so it will coat an oyster. Keep warm.

Place remaining ingredients in a pan and simmer for 5 minutes. Remove vegetables and bouquet garni. Add oysters to pan and poach over a gentle heat for 2 minutes. Drain and put oysters back in shells.

Divide oysters between 4 serving plates and coat with sauce. Garnish with lemon strips.
Serves 4

OYSTERS IN CHAMPAGNE SAUCE
Huitres au champagne

16 oysters in the half shell, scrubbed
⅔ cup dry champagne
40 g butter
1 tablespoon oil
6 shallots (spring onions, scallions), chopped
125 g fish bones
1 bay leaf
sprig thyme
⅓ cup water
½ carrot, sliced
½ stick celery, sliced
2 egg yolks
3 teaspoons brandy
½ teaspoon cornflour (cornstarch)
⅔ cup thickened (double) cream
salt and white pepper to taste
juice ½ lemon
pinch cayenne pepper
watercress, to garnish

Remove oysters from shell. Bring champagne to the boil. Reduce heat to a simmer and poach oysters for 2 minutes. Strain and reserve liquid; return oysters to shells and keep warm.

Heat butter and oil in a saucepan and cook shallots until soft but not coloured. Add fish bones, herbs, water, vegetables and reserved cooking liquid.

Bring to the boil, reduce heat and simmer for 15 minutes. Strain and reserve liquid.

Blend egg yolks, brandy and cornflour until smooth. Reheat strained liquid in pan until boiling and whisk a little into the egg yolk mixture. Stir yolk mixture into pan with remaining liquid and cook over a gentle heat, stirring constantly until sauce thickens. Off the heat, add cream very gradually or it may curdle.

Taste and adjust seasoning with salt, pepper, lemon juice and cayenne pepper. Spoon a little of the hot sauce over oysters. Place oysters under a preheated grill for 1 minute or until golden. Garnish with watercress and serve remaining sauce separately.
Serves 4

SNAILS WITH GARLIC AND PARSLEY BUTTER, BURGUNDY STYLE
Escargots à la Bourguignonne

1 litre Court Bouillon (see recipe)
1 × 220 g can escargots
400 g unsalted butter
2 cloves garlic, crushed (minced)
3 tablespoons finely chopped parsley
pinch salt
freshly ground black pepper
4 dozen empty snail shells

Bring the Court Bouillon to the boil. Add the snails, reduce heat and simmer for 10 minutes.

Combine the butter, garlic, parsley and seasonings and beat together until creamy. Remove snails from Court Bouillon and replace in their shells. Spoon a little butter on top of each snail. Place the snails into a special snail dish or shallow baking dish, placing the open end of the snail facing up so that the butter will not run out of the shell.

Bake at 200°C (400°F) for 5 minutes or until the butter is just starting to melt. Serve arranged simply on a plate.
Serves 4

Snails with Garlic and Parsley Butter, Burgundy Style

MUSSELS IN WHITE WINE
Moules marinières

1½ kg mussels
1⅓ cups white wine
80 g shallots (spring onions, scallions),
*   finely chopped*
2 bay leaves
6 peppercorns, lightly crushed (minced)
1 tablespoon chopped thyme
salt
2 tablespoons chopped parsley

Scrub mussels and remove beards. Combine all remaining ingredients except the parsley in a large saucepan and simmer for 3 minutes. Add mussels, cover and simmer a further 5–7 minutes, shaking pan occasionally. Discard any mussels which remain closed. Place mussels in soup bowls.

Strain liquid from mussels through 2 layers damp muslin. Pour liquid over mussels and sprinkle with parsley.
Serves 4–6

SCALLOPS AND MUSHROOMS IN WINE SAUCE
Coquilles St Jacques à la Parisienne

500 g scallops
1¼ cups dry white wine
few peppercorns
1 small bay leaf
4 shallots (spring onions, scallions),
*   roughly chopped*
100 g mushrooms, sliced
60 g butter
3 tablespoons flour
⅔ cup milk
2 egg yolks
⅔ cup cream
salt and pepper
lemon juice to taste
2 potatoes, cooked and mashed
½ cup Swiss cheese, grated
½ cup fresh breadcrumbs

Wipe scallops, separate roe and slice scallop meat.

Combine wine, peppercorns, bay leaf, shallots and mushrooms in a pan and bring to boil. Reduce heat and simmer for 2–3 minutes. Add scallops with enough water to cover and cook over a gentle heat for 3–5 minutes or until tender. Remove scallops and keep warm. Simmer cooking liquid until reduced to 1¼ cups and strain.

Heat 40 g of butter, add flour and cook for 2 minutes. Gradually add cooking liquid and milk. Bring to boil, stirring constantly then simmer for 5 minutes.

Combine egg yolks and cream and add ½ cup of hot sauce to cream. Gradually pour back into sauce and heat through. Do not allow to boil. Taste and adjust seasoning with salt, pepper and lemon juice.

Divide scallops between four scallop shells or individual serving dishes and cover with some sauce. Pipe mashed

Scallops and Mushrooms in Wine Sauce

potato around the edge of the dish and brush with a little milk.

Mix cheese and breadcrumbs and sprinkle over the sauce. Dot with butter and cook under a preheated grill until lightly browned and hot. Serve remaining sauce separately.
Serves 4

SCALLOP AND ASPARAGUS BOUCHÉE
Bouchée d'asperges aux coquilles St Jacques

30 g butter
12 button mushrooms, wiped, trimmed
  and sliced
2 tablespoons finely chopped shallots
  (spring onions, scallions)
¼ cup dry vermouth or dry white wine
4 scallops, rinsed and deveined
¼ cup Fish Stock (see recipe)
¼ cup cream
10 g butter blended with 2 teaspoons
  flour
12 asparagus spears, trimmed (fresh,
  frozen or canned)
1 tablespoon lemon juice
salt and pepper to taste
6 bouchée cases or 10 × 5 cm cooked puff
  pastry cases made from commercial puff
  pastry
sprigs of watercress and lemon slices, to
  garnish

Melt butter in a saucepan. Add mushrooms and gently cook until tender. Remove and set aside.

Cook shallots over a low heat until tender. Add the wine and slowly simmer. Add scallops and simmer 1–2 minutes. Remove and cover.

Simmer Fish Stock in pan until reduced by ⅓. Add the cream and continue simmering until reduced slightly. Add blended butter and flour, stirring until smooth and thickened.

Meanwhile, cook asparagus in boiling water until just becoming tender. Refresh under cold water, then drain. Cut tips from asparagus and set aside for garnish. Purée the stalks with lemon juice and seasoning to taste. Add asparagus purée to cream sauce together with mushrooms and scallops. Heat through without boiling.

Heat pastry cases at 180°C (350°F) for 10 minutes. Place on serving plates, fill with scallop mixture, arrange asparagus spears on top and garnish with watercress and a slice of lemon.
Serves 4

SEAFOOD VOL-AU-VENT
Vol-au-vent de fruits de mer

60 g button mushrooms, peeled, washed
  and diced
30 g butter
1 tablespoon lemon juice
½ cup White Wine and Shallot Sauce
  (see recipe)
parsley, chopped
salt and pepper
250 g cooked seafood (lobster, crayfish,
  crab, prawns [shrimps], mussels,
  scallops)
4 vol-au-vent cases, pre-cooked
sprigs of parsley, to garnish

Cook mushrooms in butter and lemon juice 2–3 minutes. Add White Wine Sauce, parsley and season to taste.

Spoon seafood into warm vol-au-vent cases. Serve on individual plates with sprigs of parsley.
Serves 4

Seafood Vol-au-Vent

EGGS WITH SPINACH
Oeufs Florentines

500 g silverbeet or spinach, stalks removed
40 g butter
4 eggs
¾ cup grated cheese

SAUCE
20 g butter
1 tablespoon flour
½ cup milk

Cook spinach until just tender in covered pan or in microwave oven and then drain and purée lightly in food processor or blender. Toss in 20 g melted butter over low heat for a few minutes. Arrange spinach mixture on the bottom of a shallow ovenproof dish or in 4 individual dishes.

To prepare sauce, melt remaining butter and stir in flour, cooking for 1 minute. Gradually add milk, stirring constantly until thickened and smooth. To cook in microwave oven, stir all ingredients together in a jug and cook for 1 minute. Remove to stir and cook a further 20–30 seconds if necessary.

Make holes in centre of spinach to form a nest and break an egg into each hole. Sprinkle with cheese and spoon a little sauce over each egg. Bake at 180°C for 15 minutes, until eggs are set and serve immediately with toast.

Serves 6

PARMESAN SOUFFLÉS
Soufflés à la Parmesane

2 cups milk
75 g flour
pinch salt, pepper, nutmeg and cayenne pepper
90 g grated Gruyère or Parmesan cheese
30 g unsalted butter
4 × 60 g eggs, separated
2 teaspoons milk, extra

Bring milk to the boil. Remove from heat and allow to cool slightly.

Sift flour onto a sheet of paper and add to the milk all at once. Beat vigorously with a wooden spoon until smooth. Add seasonings and return to heat. Bring to the boil and cook, stirring constantly for 5 minutes. Remove from the heat and beat in cheese, butter and egg yolks that have been lightly whisked with the extra milk.

In a clean, dry bowl, whisk the egg whites until they form soft peaks. Gently fold them into the sauce using a metal spoon. Spoon the mixture into 4 greased and collar lined, 8 cm soufflé dishes and bake at 180°C (350°F) for 10 minutes. Serve immediately.
Note: For milder flavour, use Gruyère cheese; for more bite, try Parmesan.
Serves 4

CRÊPES

⅔ cup flour
pinch of salt
2 eggs
30 g butter, melted
¼ cup milk
60 g Clarified Butter (see recipe) for frying

Sift the flour and salt. Make a well in the centre. Whisk together the eggs, melted butter and half the milk. Pour into the well and gradually blend in the flour until just combined. Overbeating results in tough crêpes. Alternatively, place the ingredients in a blender or food processor until just combined. Cover and stand the batter 1 hour. Batter can be kept 24 hours in the refrigerator.

Stir in the remaining milk until the batter is the consistency of thin cream.

Brush the pan lightly with clarified butter. Heat to very hot. Add enough batter to coat the base of the pan, turning it quickly to coat the base evenly. Cook 1 minute or until browned. Turn and brown the other side.
Note: Crêpes can be made ahead, layered between waxed paper and stored in a plastic bag. They will keep in a refrigerator for 3 days or may be deep frozen.
Serves 4

SEAFOOD AND SPINACH CRÊPES
Gâteau d'épinards et de fruits de mer

1 quantity Crêpes batter (see recipe)
30 g butter
1 onion, finely chopped
250 g uncooked prawns (shrimps), shelled (reserve shells) and chopped
250 g scallops, roughly chopped
1 × 185 g can crabmeat, drained and flaked
1 tablespoon tomato purée
salt and white pepper
1 cup thick Béchamel Sauce (see recipe)
4 egg yolks
1 large bunch silverbeet or spinach, blanched and puréed
6 egg whites

SAUCE
reserved prawn shells, crushed
1 cup dry white wine
½ cup water
salt and white pepper
1 cup thick Béchamel Sauce (see recipe)
1 tablespoon tomato purée
⅓ cup Crème Fraîche (see recipe) or cream

Use the Crêpes batter to make 7 large crêpes. Stack one on top of the other with a layer of greaseproof (waxproof) paper in between each crêpe.

Heat butter and sauté onions for 3 minutes, but do not allow to colour. Add seafood and sauté for 30 seconds. Combine seafood with tomato purée, salt, pepper, half the first cup of Béchamel Sauce and 2 egg yolks.

Combine the spinach purée with the remaining Béchamel and egg yolks. Season with salt and pepper.

Whisk egg whites to form soft peaks. Divide the egg whites between the seafood and spinach mixtures, folding through with a spatula.

Put a crêpe into the base of a well-greased 20 cm cake tin. Cover with a layer of seafood mixture, top with a crêpe, and cover with a layer of spinach mixture. Continue alternating the mixtures with a crêpe between each layer finally topping with a crêpe. Cover with foil. Bake in a bain-marie at 180°C (350°F) for 30–40 minutes or until a sharp knife inserted into the centre remains clean. Unmould the gâteau and serve in wedges accompanied with the sauce.

To prepare sauce, simmer prawn (shrimp) shells, white wine, water, salt and pepper for 20 minutes. Strain through 2 layers damp muslin, pressing hard against the shells. Simmer the liquid until reduced by half. Combine with the second cup of Béchamel, tomato purée and Crème Fraîche or cream. Heat gently.
Serves 6–8

Parmesan Soufflés

QUICHE LORRAINE

SHORTCRUST PASTRY

1½ cups flour, sifted
90 g butter, chopped
1 egg yolk
pinch salt
1 tablespoon cold water
squeeze lemon juice

FILLING

250 g rindless bacon, chopped
small knob butter
2 eggs
1¼ cups thickened (double) cream
salt, pepper and nutmeg
1 cup grated Gruyère cheese
3 tablespoons chopped chives

Rub butter into flour using fingertips until mixture resembles breadcrumbs. Mix remaining pastry ingredients and add to form a firm dough. Cover with plastic wrap and leave in a refrigerator for 30 minutes.

Roll pastry out thinly on lightly floured board and line 6 × 8 cm individual quiche tins. Prick with fork and bake blind by lining with greased greaseproof (waxproof) paper and filling with rice or dried peas. Bake at 200°C (400°F) for 15 minutes. Remove rice and paper and allow to cool.

Fry bacon in butter and drain on absorbent paper (paper towels). Whip together eggs, cream, seasoning, cheese and chives. Arrange bacon in pastry cases and fill with cream mixture. Cook 15 minutes at 200°C (400°F) and then lower temperature to 180°C (350°F) for further 10 minutes. Serve hot or cold as entrée or with a fresh salad as a main meal.
Serves 6

TARTLETS OF SEAFOOD AND WILD MUSHROOMS
Tartelettes de fruits de mer et de champignons

2 quantities of Shortcrust Pastry (see recipe) or 5 sheets ready rolled packet shortcrust pastry
60 g dried wild mushrooms
30 g butter
60 g shallots (spring onions, scallions), finely chopped
1 tablespoon Cognac or brandy
200 g cooked seafood (prawns [shrimps], crab, scallops)
150 mL Velouté Sauce (see recipe)
salt and pepper
¼ cup tasty cheese, finely grated

Roll out pastry on floured board until 3 mm thick. Cut int 6 cm rounds with a pastry cutter and press into greased, shallow patty tins. Lightly prick each with a fork and line with foil, topped with a few pieces of pasta (this weighs the pastry to inhibit rising). Bake at 200°C (400°F) for 7 minutes. Remove foil and pasta, reduce heat to 180°C (350°F) and bake tartlets again until golden.

Pour boiling water over wild mushrooms and leave to soak for 1 hour. Drain and slice. Heat butter in a saucepan and fry shallots for 3 minutes. Add wild mushrooms and Cognac and simmer for 2 minutes.

Flake crab and dice scallops and prawns. Combine seafood, Velouté Sauce, parsley and seasonings with wild mushroom mixture. Fill tartlets with mixture and sprinkle with cheese.

Warm them through in a moderate oven 180°C (350°F) for 5 minutes. Place tartlets under a moderately hot grill until golden brown.
Makes approximately 24 hors d'oeuvres

TOMATO AND SPINACH ROULADE
Roulade aux épinards et aux tomates

6 eggs, separated
6 shallots (spring onions, scallions), finely chopped
3 spinach leaves, chopped
salt and ground black pepper
¼ cup grated cheese
2 cups tomato pulp or chopped tinned tomatoes

Preheat oven to 200°C (400°F). Line a Swiss roll tin with buttered greaseproof (waxproof) paper.

Beat egg yolks until thick. Add shallots, spinach, seasoning and half the grated cheese. Whisk egg whites until stiff. Fold egg whites gently into egg yolk mixture. Spread mixture evenly in tin. Bake for 30 minutes.

Remove roulade and turn out onto a damp tea towel. Remove paper from base. Spread tomato pulp on top. Roll up inside tea towel. Remove tea towel and place roulade onto a heatproof serving platter. Sprinkle over remaining cheese.

Return roulade to oven for 2 minutes to melt cheese. Slice roulade into portions and serve with a side salad.
Serves 6

Tomato and Spinach Roulade
1 Line a tin with greaseproof (waxproof) paper

2 Fold whites into egg yolk mixture

3 Place roulade on a damp tea towel

36

4 Remove paper from base

5 Roll up roulade inside tea towel

Tomato and Spinach Roulade

SAUTÉED SWEETBREADS
Ris de veau Saint-Merard

1 pair calves sweetbreads
30 g flour
50 g butter
50 mL brandy
salt and pepper
little nutmeg
125 g button mushrooms, sliced
1 truffle, sliced
60 mL Madeira
1 tablespoon lemon juice
100 mL cream
Croûtons (see recipe)
parsley sprigs, to garnish

Wash and soak the sweetbreads for 30 minutes. Parboil them in salted water for 10 minutes. Drain and cool the sweetbreads weighted with a plate on top.

Remove the membranes, slice the sweetbreads, dip in flour and sauté in butter until golden. Pour brandy over them, ignite and flame. Season with salt, pepper and nutmeg. Add mushrooms and truffle and simmer for 3 minutes. Stir in the Madeira and simmer for 5 minutes. Add the lemon juice and cream. Heat without boiling and serve with Croûtons and parsley.
Serves 2

CATALAN STYLE LIVER
Fois d'agneau ou de veau Catalan

Here the liver is browned and lightly simmered in a well-flavoured tomato and raisin sauce. The resulting flavour is superb and will be applauded by most.

500 g calf's or lamb's liver
¼ cup flour seasoned with salt and pepper
1 tablespoon oil
1 tablespoon olive oil
300 mL Herbed Tomato Sauce (see recipe)
100 g raisins
3 tablespoons Madeira or sherry
2 tablespoons finely chopped parsley
1 tablespoon finely grated lemon zest and parsley sprigs, for garnish
1 cup Croûtons (see recipe), *for serving*

Soak the liver in cold water for 20 minutes. Pat dry with absorbent paper (paper towels) then slice into fine slivers. Dust with seasoned flour.

Heat the combined oils in a large frying pan. Add the liver and cook over a moderate heat until browned, about 5 minutes. Lift from the pan, place in an ovenproof dish and top with the tomato sauce, raisins, Madeira and parsley. Cover and bake at 180°C (350°F) for 20 minutes. Garnish with lemon zest and parsley and serve with croûtons.
Serves 4

MAIN COURSES
Plat du Jour

Fish

LEMON SOLE WITH GRAPES
Filets de sole Véronique

1 whole lemon sole or silver dory, filleted
    and skinned
40 g butter
¼ cup chopped shallots (spring onions,
    scallions)
1 bouquet garni
1 cup Fish Stock (see recipe)
salt and white pepper
125 g sultana grapes (golden raisins)
1 tablespoon Calvados or brandy
2 teaspoons flour
¼ cup dry white wine
¼ cup cream

Check fillets for bones. Roll up fillets starting with tail end, and secure with kitchen string or tooth picks.

Melt 1 tablespoon of butter in a heavy-based frying pan with a lid. Add shallots, reserving 2 tablespoons, and fry over a low heat until soft. Add bouquet garni, Fish Stock and fish. Season, cover and simmer very gently for 5–10 minutes or until the fish flakes when tested.

While fish is cooking, macerate grapes in Calvados or brandy for 15 minutes. When fish is cooked, drain, remove string and keep warm on a serving dish. Strain cooking liquid and reserve 125 mL.

In a clean pan, melt remaining butter and cook remaining shallots until soft. Add flour and cook for 1 minute, stirring. Gradually add wine off the heat then simmer until reduced by a quarter. Add Fish Stock, bring to boil then simmer for 5 minutes. Taste and adjust seasoning, stir in cream and grapes and heat through. Pour around fish.

Serves 4

FRIED STUFFED FILLETS OF SOLE
Filets de sole Villeroy

Although there are several stages in the preparation of this dish, some stages can be prepared in advance. The stock, stuffing and both sauces can be prepared the day before. Bring Velouté Sauce to room temperature before coating fillets.

4 fillets flounder or sole, skinned
salt and freshly ground pepper
15 g butter
4 button mushrooms, finely chopped
1 shallot (spring onion, scallion) finely
    chopped
½ cup fresh white breadcrumbs
½ cup white wine
⅔ cup Fish Stock (see recipe)
20 g butter
1 tablespoon flour
nutmeg, finely grated, to taste
1 egg yolk
2 tablespoons sour (dairy sour) cream
2 tablespoons oil
oil for deep-frying
¼ cup dried breadcrumbs
Herbed Tomato Sauce (see recipe)
flat leaved parsley, to garnish

Wipe fillets, check for bones and season lightly with salt and pepper.

Heat butter in a small pan, add mushrooms and shallot and cook about 3 minutes until soft. Take from the heat, add breadcrumbs and stir until combined into a stuffing.

Lay fillets, skin side up, and divide stuffing between fillets. Fold in half, with tail and head ends together and secure with sate skewers or toothpicks.

Put the fish in a lightly greased ovenproof baking dish and pour over wine and cover with a lid or foil. Cook in a preheated oven 200°C (400°F) for about 6 minutes or until fillets have firmed a little. Remove and put on a plate. Strain cooking liquid and pour into stock.

Heat butter over a low heat. Add flour and cook for 3–4 minutes, stirring constantly. Remove from heat and gradually add stock, stirring constantly. Bring to the boil, reduce heat and simmer for 5 minutes, stirring occasionally. Taste and adjust seasoning, adding nutmeg to taste.

Combine egg yolk and sour cream. Add a spoonful of hot sauce and combine. Stir mixture into sauce and cook over a very gentle heat until thick. Do not allow to boil. Cover surface of sauce with a piece of dampened greaseproof (waxproof) paper and set aside to cool.

Grease work surface with half the oil. Coat both sides of fillets with cooled sauce. Remove sate skewers, place on oiled surface and leave until cold. Beat egg with remaining oil and put on a flat plate. Place breadcrumbs on a sheet of greaseproof paper. Egg and breadcrumb fillets.

Heat oil for deep-frying 190°C (375°F). Cook fillets in oil until golden. Drain on absorbent paper (paper towel).

Serve hot, garnished with parsley and accompanied by hot Herbed Tomato Sauce.

Serves 4

Fried Stuffed Fillets of Sole

FILLETS OF SOLE WITH MUSSELS AND PRAWNS
Filets de sole à la Diéppoise

1¼ kg sole fillets (flounder)
1 kg mussels
1 cup dry white wine
60 g shallots (spring onions, scallions), finely chopped
2 bay leaves
350 g large uncooked prawns (shrimps)
100 g butter
2½ cups Fish Stock (see recipe)
1 tablespoon flour
1 cup Crème Fraîche (see recipe) or cream
3 egg yolks
white pepper
1 truffle, sliced (optional)

Scrub mussels and remove beards.

Place wine, shallots and bay leaves in pan and bring to boil. Simmer 3 minutes. Add mussels, cover and simmer 5 minutes, shaking pan occasionally. Discard any mussels which remain closed. Strain 150 mL cooking liquid through 2 layers damp muslin. Remove mussels from shells, reserving a few with shells intact for garnish.

Shell and devein prawns, leaving tails intact. Heat 30 g butter. Sauté prawns for 2 minutes, add mussels and keep warm.

Place sole fillets in a buttered, shallow baking dish. Pour the reserved, strained mussel liquid and stock over fish. Cover with foil and place in a 180°C (350°F) oven for 10 minutes or until the fish flakes easily when tested. Strain cooking liquid and keep fish warm. Boil cooking liquid until reduced by half and allow to cool slightly.

Heat 30 g butter. Add flour and cook 1 minute, stirring over a moderate heat. Off the heat, gradually blend in the reduced liquid. Bring to the boil and simmer 3 minutes, stirring continuously.

Whisk together Crème Fraîche and egg yolks. Gradually add half the hot sauce. Whisk this mixture into remaining sauce and whisk continuously over a very gentle heat until thickened. Do not boil. Soften the remaining butter and gradually whisk into the sauce, off the heat. Stir in mussels and prawns.

Pour sauce over fish and garnish with reserved mussels and sliced truffles, if desired.
Serves 6

POACHED SNAPPER
Filets de poisson à la Dugléré

1 × 1 kg whole snapper or turbot, gutted and scaled
4 tomatoes, skinned, seeded and chopped
1 onion, finely chopped
4 shallots (spring onions, scallions), finely chopped
2 tablespoons finely chopped parsley
1¼ cups Fish Stock (see recipe)
60 g butter
salt and pepper, to taste
1 tablespoon flour

TO SERVE
300 g glazed carrots sprinkled with
1 tablespoon mustard seeds
300 g zucchini (courgettes), sautéed and sprinkled with
1 tablespoon caraway seeds

Wipe fish and clean backbone rubbing with salt to remove the black membrane. If snapper is large, cut into steaks, otherwise leave whole.

Lightly grease a baking dish with butter and arrange half the tomatoes, onion and shallots on base. Place fish on a layer of vegetables and cover with remaining vegetables. Sprinkle with half the parsley then pour in stock. Lightly spread 30 g butter over the fish.

Cook in a preheated oven at 190°C (375°F) for 30 minutes or until fish flakes easily when tested. Carefully lift fish to a serving dish and keep warm.

Pour cooking liquid and vegetables into a small pan. Taste and adjust seasoning. Bring to the boil and simmer until reduced by ¼.

Combine remaining butter and flour. Gradually add mixture to pan and simmer until sauce is thickened.

Taste and adjust seasoning and pour over fish. Garnish with remaining parsley and serve with glazed carrots garnished with mustard seeds and sautéed zucchini (courgettes) garnished with caraway seeds.
Serves 4

SNAPPER QUENELLES
Quenelles

This dish requires great care, but is worth the effort.

500 g snapper fillets (pike or sole can be used)
salt and white pepper
2 egg whites
1¼ cups cream, well chilled
3 cups Fish Stock (see recipe)
Nantua Sauce (see recipe)

Skin snapper fillets and remove all bones. Purée fish in a blender or food processor. Do not overprocess. For a finer quenelle, put flesh through a drum sieve. Season lightly with salt and pepper, cover and chill in refrigerator for 1 hour.

Whisk egg whites lightly until broken down but not frothy. Gradually add egg white to the fish, a teaspoon at a time, and beat well between additions. Chill mixture, covered, for a further 30 minutes. Gradually add cream to mixture, whisking to incorporate. Return to refrigerator for a further 30 minutes.

Place Fish Stock in a frying pan and bring to the boil. Reduce heat and allow to simmer.

Using 2 wet tablespoons, shape fish mixture into ovals. Very carefully place in the stock and poach for 10–12 minutes or until cooked when tested. Using a slotted spoon, lift quenelles out of the stock and place on absorbent paper (paper towel) to dry. Remove to serving plate and serve hot with Nantua Sauce.
Serves 6

TROUT WITH ALMONDS
Truite aux amandes

4 trout
salt and pepper
75 g butter
50 g flaked almonds
juice 1 lemon

Clean the trout if necessary and wipe over with absorbent paper (paper towel). Season with salt and pepper.

Melt the butter in a large frying pan and fry the trout for 6 minutes on each side or until golden brown and cooked through. Remove trout from pan, place on a heated serving platter and set aside in a warm oven while preparing the sauce.

Add the almonds to the pan and fry until golden. Add lemon juice, mix well and serve, spooned over the fish.
Serves 4

Snapper Quenelles

1 Gradually add chilled cream to fish

2 Remove quenelles from stock

TROUT WITH RED WINE SAUCE
Truite à la Génevoise

4 trout, gutted
salt and pepper
4 tablespoons water
4 peppercorns

SAUCE
30 g butter
1 small onion, finely chopped
½ carrot, finely chopped
1 cup red wine
1 sprig fresh thyme
20 g butter
3 teaspoons flour
¼–½ teaspoon anchovy essence
1 tablespoon chopped parsley

TO SERVE
new potatoes, steamed and
snow peas (mangetout), sautéed

Preheat oven to 180°C (350°F).

Wipe trout and season lightly with salt and pepper. Grease baking dish and put the trout in with water and peppercorns.

Cover trout with a piece of buttered greaseproof (waxproof) paper and bake for about 20 minutes or until fish flakes easily when tested. Remove and keep warm on a serving plate. Strain and reserve cooking liquid.

Fish Barbecued with Fennel

Heat half the butter and sauté vegetables. Pour in wine and simmer until reduced by ½. Stir in reserved cooking liquid and thyme and simmer for a further 5 minutes.

Combine 1 tablespoon butter with the flour and add to pan in pieces.

Simmer until sauce thickens. Stir in anchovy essence, remaining butter and parsley and taste to adjust seasoning. Spoon sauce over the fish and serve hot with steamed new potatoes and sautéed snow peas.
Serves 4

FISH BARBECUED WITH FENNEL

4 red mullet or silver bream
large bunch fennel
½ cup olive oil
1 lemon, juiced
4 tablespoons Cognac or brandy
salt and ground black pepper
2 cloves garlic, crushed (minced)

Scale, gut and clean fish. Place a fennel branch inside each fish. Score fish with 3 × 5 cm long incisions in each side.

Combine oil, lemon juice, Cognac, salt, pepper and garlic. Pour over fish and marinate 1 hour.

Place fennel stalks in oven at 100°C (200°F) until dried out. Place dried fennel on the barbecue over hot coals. Barbecue fish over fennel for 5 minutes each side or until the fish flakes easily when tested. The fennel will burn, imparting an aromatic taste to the fish.
Serves 4

FISH BAKED IN PAPER
Poisson en papillote

Baking food in paper is an old cookery method used before the advent of foil. The paper retains the juices, keeping the food succulent.

4 × 250 g whole white fish
60 g butter
125 g button mushrooms
1 onion, finely chopped
8 thin slices leg ham
1 egg white, lightly beaten
¼ cup oil
Herbed Tomato Sauce (see recipe)

Preheat oven to 180°C (350°F).

Clean and wash fish. Heat butter in pan and cook mushrooms and onions for 5 minutes until softened and slightly browned.

Take 4 sheets of greaseproof (waxproof) paper, 30 × 60 cm long and fold each sheet in ½ crosswise to make a square of 30 × 30 cm.

Place a slice of ham in the centre of 1 side of each square of paper. Spread over a spoonful of cooked vegetables. Place fish on top and stuff with a little vegetable mixture. Spread a little more vegetable mixture on top then add remaining ham. Fold paper over fish and cut edges to form ½ circle or crescent shape.

Brush edges of paper with egg white to help seal them. Fold over the other side of the paper and roll up the sides to make a sealed envelope. Brush the outside of each envelope with oil.

Place envelopes on a well-oiled tray and bake in a preheated moderate oven 180°C for 20 minutes or until tender. Serve hot with Herbed Tomato Sauce.
Serves 4

SKATE WITH BLACK BUTTER
Raie au beurre noir

1 kg skate wings
2 1/3 cups Fish Stock (see recipe)
1/3 cup vinegar
150 g Clarified Butter (see recipe)
extra 2 tablespoons vinegar
1 tablespoon chopped parsley
2 tablespoons capers

TO SERVE
buttered boiled potatoes

Wipe skate wings and cut into equal serving-size pieces. Plunge skate into boiling water for 4 minutes. Cool slightly and remove skin.

Place stock and vinegar in pan and bring to boil, add skate and poach for 12 minutes or until tender. Drain well and pat dry. Place on a serving dish and keep warm.

Heat butter in pan until it is brown and foaming but not black. Sprinkle vinegar over skate then pour over the butter. Sprinkle with parsley and capers. Serve hot with buttered boiled potatoes.
Serves 4

GRILLED SARDINES IN MUSTARD SAUCE
Sardines grillées au moutarde

24 fresh sardines, scaled, boned and gutted
rock (sea) salt, ground
75 g butter
1 1/2 tablespoons flour
1 1/3 cups dry white wine
2 tablespoons Dijon-style mustard
ground black pepper
juice 1 lemon
1/2 cup fresh breadcrumbs
1 tablespoon finely chopped parsley

Cut through backbone of each sardine near the tail and remove backbone with as many other bones as possible. Sprinkle sardines with rock salt and place under moderately hot griller for 2–3 minutes each side. Place in shallow ovenproof dish.

Melt 30 g butter, stir in flour and cook, stirring for 2 minutes. Remove from heat and gradually blend in wine. Return to heat and simmer for 3 minutes, stirring continuously. Add mustard, pepper and lemon. Pour sauce over fish.

Heat remaining butter and sauté breadcrumbs until golden brown. Sprinkle over fish and bake at 210°C (425°F) for 5 minutes. Serve sprinkled with parsley.
Serves 4–6

Grilled Sardines in Mustard Sauce

1 Run fingers along sardine's backbone   2 Remove backbone and other bones

43

FISH WITH POTATOES, ONIONS AND WHITE WINE
Cotriade

2 kg assorted fish (ling, kingfish, seabream, cod, hake, etc.)
150 g butter
250 g onions, sliced
500 g new potatoes, sliced
3 cloves garlic, crushed (minced)
2 cups Fish Stock (see recipe)
2 cups dry white wine
1½ tablespoons finely chopped summer savory or thyme
salt and white pepper
1 medium breadstick
3 tablespoons flour
½ cup Crème Fraîche (see recipe) or cream

Fillet fish, removing all skin and bones and cut fillets into large pieces. Reserve heads and bones for stock.

Heat 75 g butter and sauté onions, potatoes and 2 cloves garlic for 5 minutes. Do not allow to brown. Add Fish Stock, wine, 1 tablespoon summer savory, salt and pepper and simmer 10 minutes.

Slice breadstick thinly. Rub each slice with remaining garlic. Melt 30 g butter and brush over bread. Bake at 170°C (325°F) until crisp and golden brown.

Add fish to stock and simmer 7–10 minutes or until fish flakes easily when tested.

Strain stock, placing fish and potato mixture into a large, deep serving dish. Keep warm. Bring the stock back to the boil. Blend the remaining butter with the flour to form a smooth paste. Add to the stock in small pieces, whisking continuously over a moderate heat for 3–5 minutes or until thickened. Stir in the Crème Fraîche. Heat through.

Serve Cotriade sprinkled with the remaining chopped herbs and accompanied by croûtes.
Serves 4–6

FISH IN RED WINE, BACON AND MUSHROOMS
Matelote

These hearty fish stews take their name from the boatmen of France's waterways.

Matelotes are found throughout France, each region lending its local ingredients to form its own special style of matelote.

2 kg fish (cod, snapper, whiting, conger eel, etc.)
salt and ground black pepper
2 leeks, well-washed, whites sliced
2 onions, sliced
1 carrot, sliced
1 tablespoon chopped thyme
1 tablespoon chopped parsley
3 bay leaves
1½ cups Fish Stock (see recipe)
1½ cups red wine
125 g butter
250 g baby onions
125 g bacon, cut into 3 cm strips
250 g button mushrooms
3 tablespoons flour
¼ cup oil
12 slices white bread, made into heart shapes, to garnish

Gut and scale fish. Remove and reserve heads for stock. Cut fish across the bone into thick slices. Season with pepper and salt.

Place leeks, onions, carrot, thyme, parsley and bay leaves in an ovenproof dish. Place the fish on top and pour in stock and wine. Cover with a lid or foil and bake in a 180°C (350°F) oven for 20 minutes or until the fish flakes easily when tested.

Heat 30 g butter and sauté baby onions for 5–7 minutes until golden. Remove from pan and keep warm. Wipe out pan with kitchen paper (paper towel). Add bacon to the pan and sauté 2 minutes. Add mushrooms and sauté a further 3 minutes. Add bacon and mushrooms to the onions.

When the fish is cooked, transfer fish pieces to a serving dish. Add bacon, mushrooms and onions. Keep warm.

Strain the fish liquid through a sieve. Blend 50 g butter with the flour to form a smooth paste. Bring the strained liquid to the boil. Whisk in the butter/flour mixture a little at a time. Simmer for 5 minutes, stirring occasionally. Pour over fish pieces.

Heat remaining butter and oil. Fry heart-shaped bread slices in a little oil until golden. Drain well and use to garnish the matelote.
Serves 4–6

LOBSTER THERMIDOR
Homard Thermidor

1 × 675 g lobster or crayfish, cooked
2 tablespoons grated Cheddar cheese
dash lemon juice
pinch cayenne pepper
3 teaspoons French mustard

SAUCE
25 g butter
2 tablespoons flour
1 cup milk
1 small onion, chopped
1 tablespoon chopped parsley
salt and pepper
¾ cup dry white wine

Cut cooked lobster in ½ lengthwise and clean it. Discard legs and contents of head. Remove meat from shells and cut into chunks.

Melt butter in a pan, add flour and cook for 1 minute. Stir in milk, slowly bring to boil and simmer for 1 minute, stirring continuously.

Put onion, parsley, seasoning and wine in a pan, bring to boil and simmer until onion is soft and transparent. Strain and add to white sauce, bring to boil and simmer for 5 minutes.

In a pan add half grated cheese, the lobster meat, lemon juice and cayenne and warm through.

Coat insides of shells with mustard. Pour in lobster mixture spooning sauce on top, sprinkle with remaining cheese and place under a hot grill until golden brown.
Serves 2

PARISIAN LOBSTER
Langouste Parisienne

This dish involves quite a lot of work, but for a very special occasion, and for guests who appreciate the effort involved, it is well worth the time. In France, the recipe is made with lobster, but crayfish is a perfectly acceptable substitute.

2 onions, chopped
5 carrots, diced
½ cup vinegar
1 bouquet garni
½ teaspoon black peppercorns
3 litres water
1 × 2 kg uncooked crayfish or lobster
½ medium loaf unsliced white bread
1 small turnip, peeled and diced
90 g green beans
90 g shelled peas
4 button mushrooms, chopped
60 g ham, diced
1 small gherkin, diced
1½ tablespoons capers
Mayonnaise (see recipe)
2 × 400 g cans artichoke hearts
1 mignonette lettuce, washed
1 tablespoon aspic jelly crystals
strips of eggplant (aubergine) skin
black caviar, to garnish

Lobster Thermidor

To make court bouillon, place onions and 4 carrots in a large boiler with vinegar, bouquet garni, peppercorns and about 3 litres water. Bring to the boil.

Add crayfish and simmer 20–25 minutes. Allow to cool in the liquid.

Remove crayfish from the boiler and lay belly side up on a chopping board. Using a pair of scissors, carefully cut away membrane covering tail flesh and peel it back. Gently remove the tail flesh whole and slice into 6 or 8 medallions, depending on size.

Remove crust from bread and cut it diagonally into 2 triangular blocks. Arrange crayfish with a triangle of bread under its chest and head to raise it, on a large serving dish. Wrap crayfish legs around the bread.

Place remaining carrot and turnip in boiling water and cook until tender. Drain well and refresh.

Top and tail beans and cut into pea-sized pieces. Drop beans and peas into boiling water and cook until tender. Drain well and refresh.

Place mushrooms, ham and gherkin in a bowl with vegetables and capers. Stir through enough Mayonnaise to bind the ingredients.

Drain artichoke hearts and carefully pat dry with absorbent paper (paper towel). Arrange lettuce around crayfish on serving plate, ensuring all bread is covered. Prepare aspic jelly by dissolving in 2½ cups water, following packet instructions.

Place medallions of crayfish on a wire rack. Using small star cutter or other decorative shape, cut eggplant skin into shapes. Dip into aspic and place on crayfish. Place rack over a roasting pan and spoon aspic over medallions. Allow to set.

Brush crayfish shell with remaining aspic.

Arrange medallions, in overlapping slices, down the back of the crayfish.

Carefully spoon some of the vegetable mixture into the artichoke hearts, garnish with caviar and arrange around crayfish. Serve remaining vegetable mixture separately.

Note: Pre-cooked crayfish can be used. Omit poaching the crayfish in court bouillon.

Serves 6–8

LOBSTER IN WINE, TOMATOES AND HERBS
Homard à l'Armoricaine

The ancient province of Amorique in Brittany, which lends its name to this dish, is an area renowned for lobster. The sauce can also be adapted to other crustaceans such as crabs, yabbies (crayfish) and prawns (shrimps).

3 lobster or crayfish tails
60 g butter
80 g shallots (spring onions, scallions), chopped
2 cloves garlic, crushed (minced)
750 g ripe tomatoes, peeled, seeded and chopped
1 tablespoon tomato purée
½ teaspoon sugar
2 bay leaves
1 tablespoon tarragon, chopped
salt
pinch cayenne pepper
⅔ cup dry white wine
1 tablespoon flour
90 g Clarified Butter (see recipe)
¼ cup Cognac or brandy

TO SERVE
risotto or *steamed rice*

Remove lobster meat from shells. Crush shells and chop meat into large chunks.

Heat 30 g butter. Sauté shallots and crushed shells for 2 minutes. Add garlic, tomatoes and tomato purée. Cook 5 minutes, stirring occasionally. Add the sugar, bay leaves, tarragon, salt, cayenne pepper and wine. Simmer 15 minutes.

Pass the sauce through a sieve, pressing hard to extract as much vegetable purée as possible. Simmer the sauce for 30–40 minutes or until lightly thickened.

Beat the remaining butter with the flour. Gradually whisk into the sauce over a moderate heat until thickened. Simmer 3 minutes, stirring continuously.

Heat the Clarified Butter and sauté the lobster pieces for 5 minutes or until the flesh is firm and opaque. Pour in the Cognac. Either ignite or simmer 1 minute. Transfer the lobster pieces to hot plates. Pour the sauce over the lobster pieces. Serve accompanied by risotto simmered in fish stock, or steamed rice.
Serves 4–6

CRAB SOUFFLÉ
Soufflé de crabe

1 tablespoon grated Parmesan cheese
2 × 100 g cans crabmeat
60 g butter
2 tablespoons flour
⅔ cup milk
½ teaspoon paprika
½–1 teaspoon curry powder
few drops chilli sauce
2 tablespoons cream
salt and pepper
3 egg yolks
4 egg whites

Preheat oven to 190°C (375°F).

Lightly grease a 15 cm soufflé dish and dust with Parmesan cheese.

Remove any cartilage from crabmeat and clean.

Heat 2 tablespoons of butter and sprinkle over flour and cook for 1 minute, stirring continuously. Remove from heat, gradually add milk, bring to the boil, then reduce heat and simmer, stirring for 2 minutes.

Heat remaining butter in a pan and add paprika and curry powder for 1 minute. Add crab and chilli sauce and stir to mix well.

Stir crab mixture through sauce, add cream and salt and pepper to taste. Stir through egg yolks one at a time.

Whisk egg whites until stiff. Gently fold whites into sauce. Pour into prepared dish and bake for 20–25 minutes or until well-risen and firm. Serve with a green salad.
Serves 4

SCALLOPS BRETON-STYLE
Coquilles St Jacques á la Bretonne

500 g scallops
60 g butter
6–8 shallots (spring onions, scallions) chopped
¾ cup dry white wine
salt and white pepper
2 tablespoons flour
1 egg yolk
½ cup cream

TO SERVE
cooked rice and *green salad*

Separate white body and orange roe of scallops. Heat 30 g butter and fry shallots until soft. Add scallops, wine, salt and pepper and just cover with water. Bring to boil. Cook over a very gentle heat for 3 minutes or until scallops turn white.

Drain scallops reserving cooking liquid and divide between 4 scallop dishes or other individual flameproof serving dishes. Keep warm.

Heat remaining butter, add flour and cook, stirring, for 2 minutes. Gradually pour in strained cooking liquid, stirring constantly. Bring to boil, reduce heat and simmer for 5 minutes.

Beat egg yolk lightly with a fork and pour in ¼ cup hot sauce, whisking constantly. Return egg yolk mixture to pan and heat through over a gentle heat. Off the heat, add cream very carefully as it may curdle.

Pour sauce over scallops and place under a preheated grill to brown.

Serve with rice and a green salad.
Serves 4

BRAISED SQUID WITH FRESH TOMATO SAUCE
Calmar farci à la tomate

12 small squid
2 cloves garlic
4 rolled anchovies
2 hard-boiled eggs
2 tablespoons Parmesan cheese
1 cup soft white breadcrumbs
1 tablespoon chopped Italian parsley
salt and pepper
1½ cups Herbed Tomato Sauce (see recipe)
rolled anchovies and *parsley, to garnish*

Remove heads and tentacles from hood. Remove skin from hood and flaps by pulling firmly. Flaps can be removed if desired. Using a sharp knife score the flesh into a diamond pattern taking care not to cut all the way through. Finely slice tentacles, garlic, anchovies and eggs. Add cheese, breadcrumbs, parsley and seasonings. Place filling into prepared hoods and secure with toothpicks.

Put Tomato Sauce into pan and add squid hoods. Cover with lid and simmer 20–30 minutes, turning after 15 minutes.

When serving, pour enough sauce onto serving plates to lightly cover surface. Place 2 cooked squid hoods in centre and garnish each with a rolled anchovy and finely chopped Italian parsley.
Serves 6

Braised Squid with Fresh Tomato Sauce

1   Remove heads and tentacles from
    hood

2   Remove skin from hood and flaps by
    pulling firmly

3   Score flesh in a diamond pattern
    using a sharp knife

47

Beef

STEAK TARTARE

Steak Tartare is the name given to a delicious, unusual and highly digestible dish of raw steak.

You should use fillet steak — preferably the thin tail end — but you can use sirloin or rib, both of which are very tender. Make sure the meat is absolutely fresh: locally killed beef is best. Allow 150 g meat for a generous portion per person, and make sure it is passed through a mincer twice.

600 g minced fillet steak
salt and ground black pepper
100 g shallots (spring onions, scallions),
*   finely chopped*
2 tablespoons chopped parsley
8 anchovy fillets, chopped
1 tablespoon capers
1 tablespoon gherkins (dill pickles),
*   chopped*
15 g French shallots
⅛ cup Oil and Vinegar Dressing (see
*   recipe)*
⅛ cup Mayonnaise (see recipe)
4 eggs

TO SERVE
salad

Season minced steak with salt and freshly ground black pepper. Divide it into 4 portions and shape each into a ball. Place each in the centre of a dinner plate, flatten slightly and make a small cavity in the centre.

Either surround each portion with, or serve separately, the shallots, parsley, anchovy fillets, capers, gherkins and French shallots. Serve a bowl each of Dressing and Mayonnaise.

Carefully break each egg and separate white from yolk. Leave yolk in half the shell and place in centre of each steak.

Allow your guests to help themselves to various garnishes and sauces. Serve with salad.
Serves 4

CHÂTEAUBRIAND

500 g beef fillet, cut from the thickest
*   section of the fillet*
1 tablespoon oil
freshly ground black pepper
200 g Parsley Butter (see recipe)

Steak Tartare

Steak with Green Pepper Sauce

TO SERVE
Soufflé Potatoes (see recipe)
small bunch fresh watercress

Pound the fillet slightly to form an even piece 4 cm thick. Brush the fillet with oil and season with peper.

Grill under a hot grill for 8 minutes for medium rare. Carve the fillet into thick slices and arrange on a heated platter. Place Soufflé Potatoes in the centre and serve with Parsley Butter spooned over.
Serves 2–4

STEAK WITH GREEN PEPPER SAUCE
Entrecôte au poivre vert

4 sirloin steaks, 1 cm thick
¼ cup oil
pinch salt
50 g butter
3 tablespoons brandy
½ cup dry sherry or dry Madeira wine

SAUCE
1 medium onion, chopped
2 tablespoons green peppercorns, canned
2 tablespoons soy sauce
1 teaspoon vinegar
⅔ cup cream
pinch paprika
1 tablespoon chopped parsley, to garnish

Trim steaks of any fat and sinew. Brush with a little oil and season very lightly with salt.

Heat remaining oil and butter in a frying pan and quickly fry steaks on both sides for about 2 minutes to sear flesh. Pour in brandy and set it alight. Almost immediately pour in sherry to put out brandy flames. Remove steaks and keep them warm while cooking sauce.

Add onion, peppercorns, soy sauce and vinegar to pan mixture. Boil for 4 minutes. Add cream and paprika and boil briskly for another minute.

Return steaks to sauce to reheat for a minute on each side. Serve immediately, garnished with parsley.
Note: Green peppercorns are fresh berries of the spice more commonly used in its dried form as black or white ground pepper. They are usually only available in canned form and have a mild and aromatic flavour.

Given cooking times for sirloin steak are designed for a rare-cooked steak of 1 cm thick. Thicker steaks should be fried for twice given length of time, or beaten with a rolling pin or meat mallet to given thickness. For a medium-cooked steak, fry for 4 minutes. For a well-cooked steak, cover the pan while frying for 4–5 minutes.
Serves 4

BEEF IN BRIOCHE PASTRY
Filet de boeuf en croûte

BRIOCHE DOUGH
670 g flour
2 teaspoons salt
3 teaspoons compressed yeast or 1 × 7 g
*   sachet dry yeast*
approx. ⅔ cup warm water
4 eggs
175 g softened butter

BEEF
1 kg fillet
pepper
⅓ cup oil

TO SERVE
Rich Brown Sauce (see recipe)

Sift the flour and salt onto a board reserving ¼ of the flour (this amount is used for kneading). Divide the remaining flour in ½ and form into 2 heaps. Crumble the yeast into the warm water adding 1 tablespoon flour. Set aside for 10 minutes or until starting to foam.

Make a well in the centre of 1 mound of flour and pour in yeast mixture. Start mixing using 1 hand, drawing the flour into the mixture to form a smooth, sticky dough. Place into a lightly greased bowl, cover and set aside in a warm place for 30 minutes or until doubled in bulk. Make a well in the second mound of flour and add the eggs mixing with 1 hand to form a sticky dough.

Add the egg dough to the yeast dough and beat or knead thoroughly using your hand until the mixture is very elastic. This may take 5 minutes. Gradually add the softened butter beating or kneading until incorporated.

Set aside covered in a warm place until doubled in bulk. Preheat the oven to 220° (425°F).

Season the fillet. Heat the oil in a frying pan, add the beef and cook on all sides to seal in the juices. Transfer beef and pan juices to a baking pan and roast for 15–20 minutes.

Knead the dough for 5 minutes on a lightly floured board using the reserved flour. Roll out to a rectangle shape 5 mm thick. Place the meat in the middle and brush with beaten egg. Brush the dough with beaten egg and fold over beef, making a large overlap. Form the ends into a neat shape. Place seam side down on a baking tray. Roll out any brioche scraps and cut into thin strips. Brush the loaf with beaten egg and arrange the strips across the top and sides.

Set aside in a warm place for 25 minutes and prick in 2 or 3 places.

Beef in Brioche Pastry
1 Crumble yeast into warm water

2 Fold yeast mixture into flour

3 Add eggs to second mound of flour

4 Gradually add butter to dough

Bake on the middle shelf of the oven for 15 minutes then reduce oven to 190°C (375°F) for a further 20 minutes. Remove from the oven and rest for 10 minutes before carving.

Serve with Rich Brown Sauce.

Note: The success of this dish depends on cooking the fillet for the right amount of time at the beginning. When the dough is wrapped around and the dish baked, no further heat will penetrate the meat.
Serves 6–8

5 Fold dough over beef with an overlap

50

SAUTÉED STEAK À LA BORDELAISE
Steack Sauté à la Bordelaise

2 rump steaks, trimmed of excess fat
1 tablespoon oil
salt and pepper
1 cup Bordelaise Sauce (see recipe)
bone marrow (optional)

Cut small, vertical incisions around the circumference of the steak to prevent the steak from curling as it cooks. Pat dry with absorbent paper (paper towel).

Heat oil in a large frying pan. When quite hot, add the steak and turn quickly to seal both sides. Season with salt and pepper and cook for a total of 6–7 minutes. Remove from pan and keep warm. Remove excess oil from the pan but retain the juices. Add the Bordelaise Sauce and simmer.

If using, add bone marrow and serve sauce immediately.
Serves 4

TOURNEDOS WITH BÉARNAISE SAUCE
Tournedos à la Béarnaise

6 tournedos (medallions of beef from the fillet), cut 5 cm thick
6 pieces of pork fat
salt and pepper
1 tablespoon oil
30 g butter
6 croûtes, cut the same diameter as the meat (see recipe)
1 quantity Béarnaise Sauce (see recipe)
300 g small new potatoes, boiled

Form tournedos into a neat shape and tie a piece of pork fat around each. Season with salt and pepper and brush with a little oil.

Heat the remaining oil and butter in a frying pan and fry the croûtes, turning once, until a golden colour. Remove from the pan and set aside.

Increase the heat and when the fat is starting to smoke add the tournedos. Turn quickly to brown on all sides. The total cooking time should be no more than 5 minutes. One minute before the meat has completed cooking, remove the string and pork fat. Turn the tournedos on their sides and roll in the cooking butter to sear and brown the sides.

Arrange the croûtes on a heated serving platter. Place a tournedos on each croûte and spoon a little Béarnaise Sauce over each.
Serves 6

FILLET STEAKS WITH MUSHROOM AND MADEIRA SAUCE
Tournedos chasseurs

6 tournedos (medallions of beef from the fillet), cut 5 cm thick
6 pieces of pork fat
salt and pepper
1 tablespoon oil
30 g butter
6 croûtes, cut the same diameter as the meat (see recipe)
1 cup Tomato and Mushroom Sauce (see recipe)
300 g mushrooms, sliced
30 g extra butter

TO SERVE
3 tomatoes, halved and grilled
500 g Duchess Potatoes (see recipe)

Form tournedos into a neat shape and tie a piece of pork fat around each. Season with salt and pepper and brush with a little oil.

Heat the remaining oil and butter in a frying pan and fry the croûtes, turning once, until a golden colour. Remove from the pan and set aside. Increase the heat and when the fat is starting to smoke add the tournedos. Turn quickly to brown on all sides. The total cooking time should be no more than 5 minutes. One minute before the meat has completed cooking, remove the string and pork fat. Turn the tournedos on their sides and roll in the cooking butter to sear and brown the sides.

Arrange the croûtes on a heated serving platter and place a tournedos on each.

Keep warm while preparing sauce. Melt the extra butter in the pan. Add mushrooms and cook, stirring occasionally until tender and moist. Add the Tomato and Mushroom Sauce and stir until combined. Spoon over the tournedos. Arrange the grilled tomatoes and Duchess Potatoes on the platter and serve.
Serves 6

BOEUF BOURGUIGNON

1 kg silverside cut into 2.5 cm cubes
½ cup oil
1 carrot, thinly sliced
1 large onion, thinly sliced
1 tablespoon flour
2½ cups dry red wine
salt and pepper
2 cloves garlic, crushed (minced)
1 bouquet garni
100 g small onions, peeled
1 tablespoon sugar
50 g butter
100 g streaky bacon rashers cut in strips
100 g mushrooms, chopped

Heat ¾ oil in large saucepan with pieces of beef and brown over a high heat. Remove meat, then pour out any remaining oil and add carrot and onion. Brown lightly, then add flour and cook, stirring constantly with a wooden spoon.

Add the wine, bring to boil and allow at least ⅓ to evaporate on a high heat. Return meat to pan and add enough cold water to cover. Add salt, pepper, garlic and bouquet garni. Cover and cook gently for 2½ hours.

Put small onions in a pan with sugar, butter and enough water to cover. Cover and cook until water has evaporated. When a golden caramel mixture remains, roll small onions in it and put to one side.

Heat remaining oil in a pan and lightly fry bacon. Drain and reserve. Fry mushrooms in the same oil and reserve.

When stew is cooked, sieve sauce, then return it to pan. Add small onions, bacon and mushrooms and cook for a further 10 minutes.
Serves 6

BEEF CASSEROLE IN STOUT
Carbonnade de boeuf à la Flamande

1.5 kg lean blade of beef
⅓ cup oil
3 onions, sliced
3 cloves garlic, crushed
pinch nutmeg
salt and pepper
2 tablespoons flour
1¼ cups Brown Beef Stock (see recipe)
1¾ cups stout
1 tablespoon malt vinegar
1 bouquet garni
1 tablespoon sugar

SAVOURY CRUST
1 stick French Bread
100 g butter
1 clove garlic, crushed (minced)
1 tablespoon Dijon mustard

Preheat oven to 190°C (375°F).

Cut beef into 1 cm thick slices, about 7.5 cm long and 4 cm wide. Heat oil in a frying pan and, when it begins to sizzle, add meat. Brown on all sides for 3–4 minutes. Remove and drain on absorbent paper (paper towels).

Reduce heat and add onions to pan. Stir-fry until they are golden, but do not allow to burn. Add garlic, nutmeg and seasoning and sprinkle in flour. Cook for 2 minutes. Pour in stock, stout and vinegar and stir until sauce comes to boil.

Place meat in an ovenproof casserole. Pour over sauce and add bouquet garni. Cover and cook in oven for 2¼ hours.

Cut French bread into 1 cm slices. In a bowl blend together butter, garlic and mustard. Spread this mixture thickly over one side of each slice of bread.

When casserole is cooked, remove bouquet garni and stir in sugar. Check seasoning. Cover top with slices of bread, buttered side upwards. Push bread below surface so that it is well-soaked in gravy. Return casserole to the oven and cook uncovered for another 30 minutes, so that the bread is crisp and golden.
Serve straight from the casserole.
Serves 6–8

OXTAIL STEW
Ragoût de queue de boeuf

1 kg oxtail, cut into pieces
½ cup seasoned flour
3 tablespoons oil
1 large onion, sliced
2 large carrots, cut into pieces lengthways
2 turnips, cut into chunks
3 stalks of celery, thickly sliced
1 litre water
3 beef stock cubes
2 tablespoons tomato paste
1 bay leaf
1 bouquet garni
½ teaspoon oregano
pepper to taste
1 tablespoon chopped parsley

Remove excess fat from the oxtail and toss in seasoned flour. Heat oil in a large pan and brown meat well. Remove from pan, drain on absorbent paper (paper towels) and place in a large ovenproof casserole.

Lightly fry onions, carrot and turnip pieces and celery. Drain and transfer to casserole.

In a separate saucepan, combine water, crumbled stock cubes, tomato paste, bay leaf, bouquet garni and oregano and bring to boil. Check seasoning and add a good sprinkle of pepper.

Pour this liquid over meat and vegetables. Cover casserole tightly and cook at 160°C (325°F) for 3 hours. Skim off any visible fat. If possible cool and chill overnight so that fat sets firmly and is easy to remove. Reheat before serving.
Serves 6

BEEF IN RED WINE
Boeuf à la mode

8 carrots, sliced thinly
4 onions, finely chopped
1 bay leaf
½ teaspoon thyme
3 sprigs parsley
¼ teaspoon salt
ground black pepper
1.5 kg round steak, in one piece
1½ cups red wine
2 tablespoons olive oil or vegetable oil
4 cloves garlic
12 large mushrooms, chopped
1 teaspoon lemon juice
250 g bacon
½ cup Brown Beef Stock **(see recipe)**
3 tablespoons flour

Place carrots, 1 onion, bay leaf, thyme, parsley, salt and pepper in a bowl. Add beef and wine and cover, leaving to marinate in refrigerator for 24 hours, turning every 8 hours. Remove meat. Dry on absorbent paper. Strain and reserve marinade.

Heat oil in a heatproof casserole and brown meat on all sides over high heat. Remove meat and set aside. Lower heat and fry onions and garlic in same oil for 3 minutes. Add mushrooms and lemon juice and continue cooking for 5 minutes.

In the meantime, fry bacon until almost crisp. Drain and leave to one side. Mix reserved marinade with stock and heat. Stir flour into onions and mushrooms. Add bacon. Replace beef and stir in warm wine and stock. Cover and cook 2½ hours at 180°C (350°F).
Serves 8

Veal

VEAL WITH DRIED FRUITS
Veau aux fruits d' hiver

150 g dried apricots
125 g prunes
50 g raisins
4 dried figs, quartered
50 g pistachio nuts, shelled
1 cup dry white wine or beer
Approx 750 g–1 kg boned loin or leg of
*   veal*
50 g butter
1 onion, chopped
1 clove garlic, crushed (minced)
salt and freshly ground black pepper
1 sprig fresh thyme
500 mL White Stock (see recipe)
juice and zest of 1 lemon

Marinate fruits in white wine for 1½ hours.

Tie meat evenly and brown in butter with onion and garlic. Add seasonings, thyme, stock and lemon and cook gently for 30 minutes, turning occasionally.

Drain fruits. Reserve the marinade. Add fruits to the meat. If there is insufficient liquid, add some marinade.

Replace lid and cook a further 30 minutes.

Remove meat and place in a low oven to keep warm. Boil the pan contents until the liquid has reduced by ½.

Serve meat surrounded by fruit.
Serves 4–6

Veal with Dried Fruits

BLANQUETTE DE VEAU

1 kg veal shoulder, boned and cut into
*   2.5 cm cubes*
salt and pepper
2 large carrots
1 large leek, washed and chopped
1 stalk of celery, chopped
2 cloves garlic, chopped
1 onion studded with 2 cloves
bouquet garni
80 g butter
2 tablespoons flour
500 g small white onions
250 g button mushrooms
juice ½ lemon
2 egg yolks
½ cup thickened (double) cream
pinch nutmeg

TO SERVE
noodles or rice

Place veal in a large saucepan, cover with water and bring to boil. Drain and rinse in cold water, removing any scum. Return meat to saucepan, again cover with water, season with salt and pepper and bring to boil before simmering.

Scrape and slice the carrots into 4 pieces, lengthways. Add these and leek, celery, garlic, the onion studded with cloves and bouquet garni to meat. Cover and simmer gently for 1¼ hours.

Melt half the butter in a small pan, add flour, blend and cook for 2 minutes and leave to cool. Parboil small white onions and then fry in butter until they are brown and soft. Blanch mushrooms in remaining butter with lemon juice and 2 tablespoons water. This liquid may be added to stew.

When meat is cooked, remove from pan and keep warm. Remove carrots, then strain sauce. Gradually pour about 3½ cups of this liquid into butter and flour mixture and blend well. Return to heat and continue stirring until mixture boils and sauce is thin and smooth. Adjust seasoning to taste.

In another bowl, beat together egg yolks and cream with a pinch of nutmeg. Stir in about ½ cup of unthickened stew liquid, then pour egg mixture into the thin, hot sauce, stirring briskly until sauce is thick and smooth.

Return meat, carrots, mushrooms and small onions to a pan and pour sauce over them. Reheat without bringing to boil. Place veal stew in centre of heated serving dish and surround with noodles or rice.
Serves 6

VEAL WITH APPLE AND CALVADOS
Escalopes à la Normande

6 veal escalopes
120 g butter
salt and pepper
2–3 tablespoons calvados or apple cider
½ cup cream
1 apple, peeled, cored and sliced into rings

Pat veal dry with absorbent paper (paper towel).

Melt 60 g butter over a high heat. Add veal and quickly fry until a golden brown colour on both sides. Season with salt and pepper. Add calvados and ignite and flame. When the flames die away, add cream and swill pan from side to side. Reduce heat to low and simmer for 2–3 minutes. If a thicker sauce is desired, lift veal from pan and boil sauce until reduced.

Melt remaining butter in a separate pan. Add apples and cook over a high heat for 3 minutes or until golden brown.

Spoon apples onto a heated serving dish. Place veal on top and serve with sauce spooned over.
Serves 6

CRUMBED VEAL ESCALOPES WITH BROWN BUTTER
Escalopes de veau au beurre noisette

6 × 125 g veal escalopes
salt and pepper
1 egg
3 tablespoons oil
1 cup fresh breadcrumbs
100 g unsalted butter
juice ½ lemon

Lightly pound escalopes with a mallet until they are 3 mm thick. Season with salt and pepper. Beat egg in a dish with a little salt and one tablespoon oil.

Dip veal in egg mixture then breadcrumbs. Refrigerate for ½ hour. Combine half the butter with remaining oil in a pan and heat. Add escalopes arranging them so that they don't overlap and cook over high heat to sear. Cook until browned on both sides then reduce the heat to low for 6 minutes.

Transfer veal to a heated platter. Discard oil from pan. Add remaining butter and cook until a golden, nut colour.

Squeeze lemon over veal then pour over the butter sauce. Serve immediately.
Serves 6

Veal with Apple and Calvados

ROAST VEAL STEAKS PARISIENNE
Escalopes de veau Parisiennes

1 kg loin of veal, cut in 6 steaks
salt and pepper
100 g butter
1¼ cups dry white wine
800 g potatoes, scooped into balls
250 g small onions
½ cup cream
2 slices cooked ham, diced
250 g cooked mushrooms, diced
6 cooked artichoke bottoms
chopped parsley, to garnish

Preheat oven to 200°C (400°F).

Season veal steaks and spread them with half the butter. Cook in oven for ½ hour, turning once to brown both sides. During cooking, use wine to baste meat.

Fry potato balls and onions, covered, in remainder of butter for 10 minutes. Drain and keep hot.

When meat is cooked, drain gravy into a pan and bring to boil. Add cream and boil for 5 minutes. Season to taste.

Place steaks in an ovenproof dish and pour a little sauce over. Mix ham and mushrooms and pile on top of artichoke bottoms. Arrange these around meat and place in oven for 12 minutes to heat through.

Decorate dish with potato and onions and sprinkle with parsley. Serve remaining sauce separately.
Serves 6

Lamb

LAMB AND VEGETABLE STEW
Navarin printanier

⅓ cup oil
900 g leg of lamb cut into 2.5 cm cubes
1 onion, chopped
2 tablespoons tomato paste
1 beef stock cube
1¼ cups cider
900 mL water
salt and pepper
250 g shallots (spring onions, scallions)
250 g peas
1 teaspoon sugar
15 g butter
250 g baby carrots, quartered
250 g turnips, cut in strips
¼ cup flour

Heat ¼ cup oil in a pan and brown lamb for 8 minutes. Place meat in a casserole.

In the same oil, fry onion until tender. Stir in tomato paste and cook for 1 minute. Add stock cube, cider and water and season. Boil for 10 minutes.

Pour sauce over meat. Cover and simmer for 1½ hours.

Boil shallots and peas until tender in water seasoned with salt, pepper and half the sugar. Drain, toss in butter and keep warm.

Boil carrots and turnips separately in water seasoned as for peas and onions and drain.

Mix remaining oil and flour over a low heat for 3–4 minutes. Add a little of the gravy, stir and simmer for 10 minutes.

Pour into stew and stir on a low heat for 5 minutes.

Serve the vegetables in a separate dish to the lamb.
Serves 6

HARICOT BEAN LAMB STEW
Haricot de mouton

25 g lard (shortening)
2 rashers bacon, diced
8 button onions
550 g stewing lamb, diced
1 clove garlic, crushed (minced)
¼ cup flour
3¾ cups stock
salt and pepper
bouquet garni
225 g dried haricot beans, soaked overnight

1 carrot, chopped
1 large onion, chopped
1 tablespoon tomato paste
1 tablespoon vinegar
1 tablespoon chopped parsley, to serve

Heat lard in a pan and add bacon (keep bacon rind to cook with beans) and button onions. Colour slightly and remove from pan.

In same pan, brown meat. Drain off half fat, add garlic and flour and stir for 1 minute.

Add stock and bring to boil. Season, skim off any scum. Add bouquet garni, cover with a lid and simmer for 1½ hours.

Preheat oven to 180°C (350°F).

Drain soaked haricot beans, reserving liquid. Put beans in clean water and bring to boil. Throw water away. Put beans in ovenproof dish with carrot, onion, bacon rinds, tomato paste and vinegar. Add stock to cover and bake in oven for 1 hour or until the beans are cooked. When beans are tender, remove bacon rinds and season with salt and pepper.

To serve, either combine beans with meat in one dish, or serve separately sprinkled with parsley.
Serves 4

SPRINGTIME SADDLE OF LAMB
Selle d'agneau printanière

1.25 kg saddle of lamb
salt and pepper
75 g butter
250 g French beans
12 asparagus spears
225 g small carrots
1 teaspoon sugar
3 small onions, peeled
255 g peas
450 g new potatoes
sprig mint
6 tomatoes, skinned
2 celery stalks, cut into 4 cm lengths
1 tablespoon chopped parsley, to serve

Preheat oven to 200°C (400°F).

Place saddle in a roasting pan. Season with salt and pepper and smother with 50 g of butter. Roast for ½ hour then reduce to 180°C (350°F) for 40 minutes, basting from time to time.

Meanwhile, top and tail French beans. Scrape asparagus and tie in bundles.

Put carrots in a saucepan with sugar and onions, and cover with water. Boil for 15 minutes. Add peas and cook for 8 minutes until water has almost evaporated. Add remaining butter. Remove from heat.

Boil new potatoes with mint until cooked and drain. Mix with carrots and peas, season with salt and pepper and sprinkle with parsley. Add tomatoes and keep warm.

Boil asparagus in salted water for 8 minutes or until tender, drain, remove string, and keep warm.

Boil celery in salted water for 15 minutes, drain and keep warm.

When ready to serve, arrange saddle on a large dish and surround with all the vegetables. Sprinkle with parsley.
Serves 4

HERBED RACK OF LAMB
Carré d'agneau persillé

6-rib rack of lamb, trimmed
2 tablespoons chopped parsley
1 tablespoon chopped shallots (spring onions, scallions)
1 small clove garlic, crushed (minced)
1 teaspoon finely chopped rosemary
½ cup fresh breadcrumbs
20 g melted butter
salt and pepper
20 g butter (extra)
watercress, to ganish

Combine parsley, shallots, garlic, rosemary, breadcrumbs and butter in a bowl.

Sprinkle lamb with salt and pepper. Melt a knob of butter in a pan and brown lamb evenly all over.

Cover lamb with herb mixture and place in a baking dish. Bake at 220°C (425°F) 15 minutes. Remove and keep warm for 10 minutes.

Slice into individual chops. Arrange 2 chops in heart shape on plates. Serve with pan juices and watercress for garnish.
Serves 2

Herbed Rack of Lamb

Lamb Provençale-style

POT ROAST LAMB
Gigot d' agneau à la Bretonne

pepper
2 kg leg of lamb, boned, rolled, tied and
trimmed of excess fat
2 cloves garlic, chopped
50 g butter
2 tablespoons oil
3 carrots, sliced
3 onions, sliced
3 leeks, sliced
2 cups Brown Beef Stock (see recipe)
450 g cooked flageolet or lima beans
1 ½ cups water
1 tablespoon cornflour (cornstarch)

Season leg of lamb and insert garlic into
cuts in flesh.

Heat 25 g butter and the oil in a casserole and brown the lamb all over for 8
minutes. Remove. Brown carrots, onions
and leeks in same fat for 5 minutes. Pour
off fat. Return lamb to casserole. Add
stock and bring to boil and simmer for 2
hours.

Reheat beans in remaining butter and
season with salt and pepper. Keep warm.

When meat is cooked, remove from
casserole and keep warm. Pour or spoon
off fat, add 1¼ cups of water and boil for
5 minutes. Thicken with cornflour mixed
with water. Boil for 5 minutes, strain and
season.

To serve, slice meat and arrange on a
dish, surrounded by beans.
Serves 8

LAMB PROVENÇALE-STYLE
Noisettes d' agneau à la Provençale

6 lamb noisettes, boned
PROVENÇALE SAUCE
225 g onions, sliced
1 clove garlic
1 tablespoon oil
1 teaspoon flour
1 tablespoon tomato paste
⅔ cup stock

225 g tomatoes, skinned, seeded and
chopped
bouquet garni
salt and pepper

TO SERVE
boiled baby potatoes

Tie lamb noisettes into a neat shape using
string. In a frying pan gently fry sliced
onion and clove of garlic for 5 minutes in
1 tablespoon of oil. Sprinkle on flour and
cook for 1 minute. Stir in tomato paste
and stock and simmer for 10 minutes.
Add tomatoes, bouquet garni and seasoning and simmer for 15 minutes until sauce
is thick. Remove bouquet garni and check
seasoning.

Season noisettes with salt and pepper
and fry for 12–15 minutes in remaining
oil. When cooked, remove sticks or string.

To serve, place sauce on a dish and put
noisettes on top. Serve with potatoes.
Serves 3

58

Pork

PORK IN CIDER
Côtelettes de porc au cidre

6 pork cutlets
½ cup oil
2 carrots, diced
2 onions, diced
1 clove garlic
2 shallots (spring onions, scallions),
  chopped
1 stick celery, thinly sliced
½ cup flour
3 tomatoes, skinned and chopped
1 cup dry cider or apple juice
bouquet garni
250 g canned corn kernels
salt and pepper

TO SERVE
1 tablespoon chopped parsley
boiled new potatoes

Heat half the oil in a saucepan and gently fry carrots, onions, garlic, shallots and celery until tender. Sprinkle in half the flour, stir and cook for 1 minute. Add tomatoes and cider. Continue stirring and bring to boil. Add bouquet garni and corn kernels and season with salt and pepper. Simmer for 15–20 minutes.

Coat cutlets in remaining (seasoned) flour and heat the rest of the oil in a pan. Shallow-fry cutlets for about 10 minutes until browned on both sides. Transfer cutlets to an ovenproof dish. Pour over the sauce and check seasoning. Cover and bake in a moderate oven for about 30 minutes or until cutlets are tender. Sprinkle with parsley and serve with boiled new potatoes.
Note: White wine may be substituted for cider or apple juice.
Serves 6

PORK WITH ROSEMARY
Daube de porc au romarin

125 g butter
1 kg lean boned shoulder or loin of pork in
  one piece
salt and pepper
1 carrot, sliced
1 large onion, chopped
1 stalk celery, diced
375 g mushrooms, thickly sliced
1¼ cups water
½ cup dry white wine
2 sprigs fresh rosemary
1 clove garlic, crushed (minced)

Melt half the butter in a flameproof casserole. Add seasoned meat and brown on all sides. Remove casserole from heat. In a separate pan heat remaining butter and sauté carrots for 5 minutes. Add onion and celery and sauté for a further 5 minutes. Finally add mushrooms, cover pan and cook on a low heat for 2 minutes.

Pour contents of pan into casserole. Add water and wine, 1 rosemary sprig and garlic. Check seasoning. Cover casserole and cook at 180°C (350°F) for 1½ hours or until meat is well cooked.

Serve garnished with the second sprig of rosemary.
Serves 6

PORK CRÉPINETTES WITH BUTTER-FRIED APPLES
Crépinettes de porc aux pommes

375 g pork mince
375 g veal mince
¾ cup fresh breadcrumbs
grated lemon rind
1 teaspoon nutmeg
salt and pepper
½ tablespoon thyme
1 teaspoon marjoram
thin sheet pork back fat

TO SERVE
2 cooking apples, peeled and sliced
30 g butter

Mix meats, breadcrumbs, lemon rind, seasonings and herbs together. With floured hands, roll portions of mixture into oval shape. Flatten slightly, then wrap each in a 2 cm square of pork back fat. Press it gently into place and secure with toothpicks.

Fry crépinettes in small amount of oil. Brown on both sides. Serve crépinettes with apple slices fried in butter.
Serves 6

Pork with Rosemary

Offal

VEAL KIDNEYS IN RED WINE
Rognons de veau Bordelaises

60 g butter
3 tablespoons flour
1¼ cups red wine
¾ cup Brown Beef Stock (see recipe)
salt
12 peppercorns, crushed (minced)
1 clove garlic, crushed (minced)
pinch thyme
1 bay leaf
2 carrots, finely chopped
4 onions, finely chopped
6 sprigs parsley, chopped
2 celery sticks, finely chopped
675 g veal kidneys, soaked in 2 changes of
*   water for 1 hour*
¼ cup oil
chopped parsley, to garnish

Put 40 g butter in a heavy-based saucepan and cook gently without colouring for 2 minutes. Sprinkle on flour and stir for 1 minute. Add ½ cup of red wine and the Brown Beef Stock. Bring to boil and season with herbs. Add carrots, half the onions, parsley and celery and simmer for 30 minutes until vegetables are tender.

Prepare kidneys by removing skin from outside, cutting off any fat, and central core. Slice into bite-sized pieces.

Heat oil in a frying pan, and sauté kidneys for 5 minutes. Remove and discard cooking fat and juices.

Heat remaining butter in a heavy-based saucepan, gently fry remaining onions and add the rest of the wine. Boil until almost evaporated.

Add cooked vegetables and sauce and simmer together for 5 minutes. Sieve sauce through a conical strainer, pressing cooked vegetables through the holes. Some cellulose will remain.

Pour over kidneys and reheat without boiling. Put in a serving dish and sprinkle with parsley.
Serves 4

ARMAGNAC FLAMBÉED KIDNEYS
Rognons flambés à l'Armagnac

4 calf's kidneys, soaked in 2 changes of
*   water for 1 hour*
2 tablespoons vinegar
1 cup water
¼ cup flour
salt and pepper

75 g butter
1 small onion, chopped
⅓ cup Armagnac or brandy
⅓ cup white wine
¼ cup thickened (double) cream
1 teaspoon Dijon mustard
juice ½ lemon
croûtes, to serve
1 teaspoon chopped parsley, to garnish

Prepare and slice kidneys thinly. Drain and dry kidneys then dredge slices in seasoned flour.

Heat butter in a frying pan and sauté kidneys and onion for about 5 minutes. Pour in Armagnac and set alight. To extinguish flames, pour in white wine. Simmer for 5 minutes. Strain off juices into a saucepan. Keep kidneys warm. Bring juices to boil and stir in cream. Boil for 2 minutes.

In a bowl, blend together mustard and lemon juice. Remove sauce from heat and stir in mustard mixture, a little at a time. Check seasoning and add kidneys.

Heat through, without boiling, and serve on croûtes sprinkled with parsley.
Serves 4

SWEETBREADS IN CREAM SAUCE
Ris de veau à la crème

4 calf's sweetbreads
pinch salt
juice 2 lemons
2 tablespoons flour, seasoned
40 g butter
100 g mushrooms, diced
1 egg yolk
2 tablespoons cream

Soak sweetbreads in cold salted water for about 3 hours, changing water from time to time. Place in a pan, cover with cold water and add a pinch of salt and half lemon juice. Bring to boil, then simmer gently for 8 minutes. Cool sweetbreads under running water and when cold, carefully pick out gristle and membranes. Dry on absorbent paper (paper towel).

Cut each sweetbread to make 4 thin slices. Dredge with flour. Heat butter in a frying pan, add sweetbreads and fry lightly until they are golden-brown on each side. Add mushrooms and fry for 2 minutes more, then lower heat, cover and cook for 15 minutes, until tender. Remove and keep hot.

Place egg yolk and cream in a bowl and beat well together. Pour remaining lemon juice into pan and heat through for 2 minutes, scraping bottom of pan with a wooden spoon to incorporate sweetbread and mushroom juices. Remove from heat, stir in cream mixture, check seasoning and pour over sweetbreads.
Serves 4

Armagnac Flambéed Kidneys

1 Skin kidneys; cut out core and fat

2 Soak kidneys in vinegar and water for 30 minutes

3 Drain and dry kidneys and dredge in seasoned flour

60

Sautéed Chicken with Mushrooms

Poultry and Game

Chicken

SAUTÉED CHICKEN WITH MUSHROOMS
Poulet sauté chasseur

1.25 kg chicken pieces
1 cup flour seasoned with salt and pepper
2 tablespoons oil
30 g butter
250 g mushrooms, chopped
3 shallots (spring onions, scallions), chopped
½ cup brandy
½ cup dry white wine
425 g peeled tomatoes, strained and chopped
sprig tarragon, chopped
1¼ cups Chicken Stock (see recipe)

Preheat oven to 180°C (350°F).

Roll chicken in seasoned flour. Combine oil and butter in a pan. Add chicken pieces and brown on all sides for about 10 minutes. Remove chicken from the pan and set aside on absorbent paper (paper towel). Place in a low oven to keep warm.

Add mushrooms to the pan and cook until tender. Add shallots, reduce the heat and cook for 1 minute.

Pour in brandy and wine, stirring to scrape any residue from the bottom of the pan. Add tomatoes, tarragon and stock and boil for 10 minutes or until the liquid has reduced. Adjust seasonings to taste.

Arrange chicken pieces in a casserole and spoon sauce over the chicken. Bake 1 hour and serve.
Serves 4

PAN-FRIED CHICKEN IN CREAM SAUCE
Poulet sauté à la crème

1.5 kg chicken
salt and pepper
2 tablespoons oil
50 g butter
350 g mushrooms, trimmed
3 shallots (spring onions, scallions), chopped
½ cup dry white wine
1 egg yolk
juice ½ lemon
pinch ground nutmeg
3 tablespoons flour
1¼ cups thickened (double) cream
¾ cup Cheddar cheese, grated

Preheat oven to 220°C (425°F).

Cut up chicken into serving-sized pieces and season with salt and pepper. Put half the butter and all the oil in a frying pan and heat. Then add chicken pieces and sauté for about 10 minutes on each side.

Add mushrooms to same pan and fry for 5 minutes. Add shallots and heat on low for 2 minutes until soft.

Pour white wine and stir, scraping bottom of pan to dissolve cooking juices, then reduce liquid to about ½ over a high heat.

Put egg yolk into a cup and mix it with lemon juice and nutmeg. Using a fork work the rest of the butter thoroughly with flour on a plate. Add kneaded butter to the sauce bit by bit, whisking vigorously and boil for 1 minute.

Add egg and lemon mixture gradually, still whisking, without letting it boil. Stir in cream.

Arrange chicken pieces in a heated ovenproof serving dish. Coat them with cream sauce. Sprinkle with grated cheese and put dish in the oven to brown. When golden and bubbling on top, serve.
Serves 4

CHICKEN BREASTS COOKED IN GREEN PEPPERCORNS
Suprêmes de volaille au poivre vert

4 whole chicken breast fillets
3 tablespoons pistachio nuts, coarsely chopped
4 slices German cream pepper cheese
1 tablespoon lemon juice
salt and pepper
30 g butter
3 slices cooked smoked ham, cut into fine strips, 5 × 5 cm
2 tablespoons canned green peppercorns, rinsed, drained and loose skins discarded
¾ cup thickened (double) cream
1 teaspoon cornflour (cornstarch)
2 tablespoons sour (dairy sour) cream

Open chicken breasts and flatten a little with a meat mallet. Place ½ tablespoon pistachio nuts along one section of each breast and place slice of cheese on top. Fold fillet over to encase stuffing. Shape and secure with toothpicks.

Place in greased baking dish and sprinkle with lemon juice, salt and pepper. Lightly glaze with half the butter, cover with aluminium foil and bake at 110°C (225°F) for 15–20 minutes. Turn off oven.

Drain cooking juices from chicken into a saucepan. Replace foil over chicken and return to oven with door ajar to keep warm.

Combine ham and peppercorns and heat gently in a pan with remaining butter. Remove from pan.

Reduce cooking juices in pan to 1 tablespoon and strain. Mix cornflour with thickened cream and blend into cooking juices. Cook sauce over moderate heat (without boiling) until thickened, add ham and peppercorns. Blend in sour cream. Spoon sauce over chicken and serve.
Serves 4

ROAST CHICKEN WITH TARRAGON
Poulet à l'estragon

1 × 1.6 kg chicken
salt and freshly ground pepper
90 g butter
1 teaspoon dried tarragon
1 onion, quartered
½ cup warm Chicken Stock (see recipe)

Preheat oven to 180°C (350°F).

Pat chicken dry with absorbent paper (paper towel) and season the cavity and skin with salt and pepper.

Beat the butter until soft, add tarragon and spread over the chicken cavity and skin, particularly the breast and leg sections.

Place onion into base of baking dish. Add chicken and bake in preheated oven for 1½ hours or until tender. Baste occasionally with pan juices and stock. Serve hot or refrigerate and serve cool.
Serves 4

COQ AU VIN

2 kg chicken pieces
2 tablespoons seasoned flour
40 g butter
125 g bacon rashers cut in strips
2 small carrots, peeled and sliced
12 shallots (spring onions, scallions)
20 g butter (extra)
½ cup brandy
2 tomatoes, skinned, seeded and chopped
1 clove garlic, crushed (minced)
1½ cups red wine
1 tablespoon chopped parsley
½ teaspoon dried thyme
1 bay leaf
salt and pepper
250 g button mushrooms

Wash and dry chicken pieces and toss in flour seasoned with salt and pepper.

Heat butter in a heavy flameproof saucepan and fry bacon strips until lightly browned. Add carrots and whole shallots and fry until golden brown. Remove with a slotted spoon and drain on absorbent paper (paper towel).

Add extra tablespoon of butter to pan, heat and fry chicken pieces until browned on all sides. Warm brandy, pour over chicken and set alight. When finished flaming, add tomatoes and garlic and cook for a few minutes. Return bacon strips, onions and carrots to pan. Pour in red wine, add parsley, thyme and bay leaf and bring to boil, stirring continuously. Add salt and pepper to taste, then cover and simmer over low heat for 45 minutes.

Wipe mushrooms, trim stalks and add to casserole. Continue cooking a further 15 minutes or until chicken is tender.

Remove bay leaf, taste and adjust seasoning to taste. Serve hot straight from the casserole.
Serves 6

Roast Chicken with Tarragon

CHICKEN CHAUDFROID
Chaudfroid de volaille

*2 small or 1 large roasting chicken, with
  giblets*
2 litres water
1 leek, sliced
1 carrot, sliced
2 sticks celery, sliced
1 bouquet garni
salt and pepper

CHAUDFROID SAUCE
50 g butter
½ cup flour
1¼ cups cream
¼ cup powdered aspic (savoury gelatine)
salt and white pepper
pinch nutmeg
½ cup dark sherry
sprig tarragon

TO SERVE
lettuce leaves
cucumber slices
tomatoes
green capsicum (peppers), sliced

Wash chicken and giblets to remove all
traces of blood. Place chicken in a large
saucepan (side by side if using 2 birds) and
cover level with water.

Parboil giblets without liver in a pan of
salted water for 5 minutes. Refresh in cold
water, drain and add to the chicken.

Add sliced leek, carrot and celery to
chicken, together with bouquet garni.
Season with salt and pepper and bring
liquid to boil gently. Simmer for 45 minutes. Remove pan from heat and cool
chicken in liquid until both are completely
cold. Take out chicken and chill in a
refrigerator for at least 4 hours.

Reboil pan of giblets, vegetables and
liquor for 1 hour to concentrate flavour,
then strain and reserve liquor.

To make Chaudfroid Sauce: melt butter in a saucepan, stir in flour and cook for
2 minutes until it has a sandy texture.
Gradually stir in 1¼ cups reserved liquor,
whisking gently to form a smooth sauce.
Pour in cream and season to taste.

Dissolve ½ aspic powder in hot sauce,
stirring all the time. Season with salt,
white pepper and nutmeg and simmer for
15 minutes, then strain through a fine
sieve.

To make the aspic: pour 1¼ cups
remaining reserved liquor into a saucepan
with ½ cup dark sherry and a sprig of
tarragon. Boil for 2 minutes then remove
tarragon and refresh in cold water, drain
and place all leaves in a dish. Dissolve
remaining aspic in tarragon stock, simmer
for 5 minutes and set aside until cold.

To decorate, place chicken(s) on a cool-
ing rack over a deep tray. Remove skin

and carve into 4 portions. Discard
unwanted bones and be sure to cut
knuckle bones from legs.

Coat each piece of chicken with warm
Chaudfroid Sauce (if it is too stiff, thin it
down with a little stock). Chill chicken in
refrigerator for 20 minutes to set sauce,
then decorate each piece with 2 tarragon
leaves.

Glaze chicken with a little semi-
thickened aspic, leave to firm, then carefully lift onto a serving dish, using 2 spat-
ulas. Decorate with lettuce leaves, cucumber slices, tomatoes and slices of green
capsicum.

Pour the rest of the aspic into an
oblong tray 3 cm deep and allow to set.
When firm, cut aspic jelly with a knife
into geometrical shapes or dice. Place aspic
jelly round the dish.
Note: If you use a boiling fowl or capons
for this dish, the breast can be sliced into
thin escalopes after cooking and each slice
coated with Chaudfroid Sauce. Instead of
tarragon, you could substitute 3–4
drained, canned asparagus tips; place them
on top of each chicken piece, securing
them in position with a little semi-
thickened aspic jelly.
Serves 4–8

Duck

NORMANDY DUCK
Canard sauté à la Normande

2 kg duck, oven-ready
50 g butter
1 medium onion, chopped
3 rashers streaky bacon, diced
1 clove garlic, chopped
700 g dessert apples, peeled and quartered
2 cups dry cider
⅔ cup thickened (double) cream
salt and pepper
2 tablespoons apple brandy

Preheat oven to 180°C (350°F).

Wash, dry and cut the duck into serving pieces and wipe.

Heat butter in a frying pan, add duck
and sauté gently for about 30 minutes or
until well-browned, covered with a lid.
Add legs 10 minutes before breasts as they
need extra cooking time.

Remove duck from pan and keep
warm. Fry onion and bacon with garlic
until golden then add apple quarters.
Cook gently for a further 2–3 minutes,
with the lid on.

Put half apple quarters in a casserole
and arrange duck pieces on top. Pour in
cider, place remaining apple pieces around
duck, cover and cook in oven for 1½
hours.

Boil cream in a pan for 2 minutes. Add
duck gravy and boil down for 5 minutes
more. Check seasoning, pour sauce over
duck in pot, stir in apple brandy and serve.
Serves 4

DUCK WITH ORANGE
Canard à l'orange

75 g butter
2 kg duck, trussed and flesh pricked
2 onions, sliced
4 carrots, peeled and sliced
3 cups dry white wine
1 bouquet garni
salt and pepper
2 oranges
1 tablespoon cornflour (cornstarch)
juice of 2 oranges
1 teaspoon caster sugar

Melt the butter in a large casserole dish.
Add duck, onions and carrots and cook
over a medium-high heat until well-
browned.

Add wine, bring to boil then reduce
heat to simmer. Cook for 10 minutes or
until wine has reduced slightly. Add bouquet garni, salt and pepper. Simmer for
1½ hours or until duck is tender. Peel
oranges thinly so that there is no white
pith. Using a sharp knife, cut into fine
strands, blanch for 4 minutes then drain.

Cut oranges into segments discarding
any membrane. Lift duck from saucepan
and divide into serving pieces. Cover with
foil and keep warm in a low oven while
preparing the sauce. Gently tilt casserole
and pour or spoon off as much fat as possible from on top of cooking liquid. Blend
a little liquid with cornflour to make a
smooth paste then return to remaining
cooking liquid.

Simmer until thickened, stirring
occasionally; remove from heat adding
orange juice, sugar and orange rind.

Place duck on a warmed serving platter
and pour over the sauce. Garnish with
orange segments and serve immediately.
Serves 6

Duck with Orange

BALLOTINE OF DUCK IN RED WINE
Ballotine de canard à la Bourguignonne

A ballotine is a piece of meat, fowl, game or fish which is boned, stuffed and rolled into the shape of a bundle.

2.5–3 kg duck, with its liver
salt and pepper
50 g butter
2 large onions, chopped
300 g sausage meat
2 cloves garlic, crushed (minced)
½ cup oil
250 g lean belly of pork, diced
250 g button onions, peeled
250 g mushrooms, quartered
1 teaspoon sugar
1 bouquet garni
3 cups good red wine
2½ cups Chicken Stock (see recipe)
1–2 tablespoons cornflour (cornstarch)
2–3 tablespoons cold water
chopped parsley, to garnish

TO SERVE
French beans or noodles

Bone duck and prepare as for a ballotine by removing flesh from skin, taking care not to split the skin. When bones are removed, lay duck out flat, remove any excess fat, then sprinkle with salt and pepper.

Melt butter in a small saucepan and cook onions for 10 minutes over a slow heat. Let them cool.

Wash liver and chop finely before putting into a bowl with sausage meat, garlic, cooked onions, salt and pepper. Mix with a wooden spoon until mixture is blended. Spread boned duck on your work surface, skin side down. Put stuffing in middle. Fold duck over it and stitch up to secure the stuffing.

Heat oil in a heavy flameproof casserole. When very hot, put in ballotine, then pork dice to brown. Stir and add button onions and mushrooms. Let them brown over low heat, adding sugar, bouquet garni and red wine. Bring to boil and reduce to about half volume.

When wine has reduced, baste ballotine with stock, season with salt and pepper and cover. Cook for 1½ hours over a slow heat.

Drain ballotine, pork dice, onions and mushrooms and keep them warm on a heated serving dish. Skim off fat with a small ladle or spoon. Pass juice through a fine mesh sieve into a pan and return to a brisk heat. Boil it down by ⅓.

Mix cornflour with cold water in a bowl. Slowly add this to reduced gravy, stirring constantly until sauce thickens and is smooth. Season to taste.

Untie ballotine and transfer to a hot serving dish. Cut into portions, then coat with sauce. Sprinkle with chopped parsley and serve immediately, with French beans or noodles.
Serves 6–8

Quail

BRAISED QUAIL WITH GRAPES
Cailles aux raisins de muscat

6–8 quails
ground black pepper
6–8 slices pork fat
40 g butter
125 g seedless white grapes, washed
fresh grape vine leaves, washed (optional)
2 tablespoons brandy

Preheat oven to 200°C (400°F).

Wipe quails and season with pepper. Cover the breast with pork back fat then truss with fine string. Heat butter in a flameproof dish and brown birds lightly.

Place dish in oven and cook, uncovered, for 8–10 minutes. Remove trussing string and pork fat and add grapes. Return quail to oven for a further 5 minutes or until cooked when tested; baste well.

Place vine leaves on individual plates and arrange quail on top. Add brandy to cooking liquid and heat through, on top of the stove, stirring well. Spoon grapes and cooking liquid over quails and serve.
Serves 6–8

QUAIL WITH WILD RICE
Cailles au riz sauvage

9 quails, 1½ quails per serve
STUFFING
20 g butter
2 shallots (spring onions, scallions), finely chopped
liver and heart of quails, diced
1½ cups wild rice, cooked
1 large red apple, cored and diced
2 tablespoons cream
1 egg yolk
salt and pepper to taste
pinch lemon thyme
MIREPOIX
(Mixture used in meat, fish and shellfish dishes to enhance their flavour.)

20 g butter
2 shallots (spring onions, scallions), chopped
1 small carrot, diced
1 small stick celery, diced
SAUCE
8 dried juniper berries marinated 2–3 hours in
3 tablespoons Madeira
1½ cups Chicken Stock (see recipe)

To make stuffing: melt butter in a pan, add shallots and cook until softened. Add liver and heart of quails and cook 5 minutes. Mix in cooked wild rice and diced apple and bind all ingredients together with cream and egg yolk. Season to taste.

To make Mirepoix: melt butter in a pan, add vegetables and cook until tender. Spoon into an ovenproof dish.

To debone the quails: lie them on their backs and starting at the tail end, make an incision along breast. Carefully remove all small bones from breast and back sections, leaving legs intact.

Spoon stuffing into cavity then stitch incision with cotton. Arrange quails in ovenproof dish in one layer. Roast at 200°C (400°F) for 15–20 minutes basting frequently. Lift quails from dish and keep warm. Remove cotton stitches.

Discard vegetables, reserving pan juices in a small saucepan. Add juniper berry mixture and Chicken Stock. Over medium heat, bring sauce to boil, add Madeira and reduce. Season to taste before straining. Spoon sauce over quail before serving.
Serves 6

Goose

GOOSE AND MUTTON CASSEROLE WITH HARICOT BEANS
Cassoulet

1 kg dried haricot beans
2 carrots, thinly sliced
1 onion, studded with 2 cloves
3 large onions, peeled
2 cloves
4 cloves garlic, peeled
500 g belly of pork
150 g bacon rinds
1 knuckle of pork
salt and pepper
800 g Preserved Goose and its fat (see recipe)

A bouquet garni enhances flavour in French casseroles

600 g chipolatas (link sausages) made with beef and pork or herbs, sliced
700 g breast of mutton, chopped
3 tablespoons tomato paste
1 bouquet garni
¾ cup dried breadcrumbs

Preheat oven to 220°C (425°F).

The day before they are needed, wash haricot beans and soak for 7–8 hours in cold water.

Drain beans and put in a large pan. Add carrots, the onion studded with cloves and 1 other onion, two cloves of garlic, belly of pork, bacon rinds and knuckle of pork. Cover with a generous amount of cold water to completely cover.

Bring water gently to boil, reduce to simmer and skim off froth. Simmer covered for 1½ hours or until beans are tender. Season with salt and pepper after about 1 hour's cooking. Reserve cooking liquid.

Chop remaining 2 onions and crush (mince) remaining garlic.

In a casserole, heat 2 tablespoons of fat from preserved goose. Fry chipolatas until brown then remove from pan. In same fat, fry mutton pieces until browned.

Add chopped onions and crushed garlic and cook until soft. Replace sausage slices in pan. Add tomato paste and bouquet garni and season with salt and pepper.

Add to pan 1 cup of cooking liquid from the haricot beans. Cover and simmer on a low heat for about 1½ hours.

Thirty minutes before haricot beans have finished cooking, remove carrots and clove onion and add sausage and mutton, together with their sauce, and preserved goose meat.

When beans are cooked, drain contents of pan and dice belly of pork and bacon rind. Correct seasoning if necessary. Arrange in a fairly deep earthenware dish, alternate layers of different meats and beans. Finish with a layer of beans.

Sprinkle breadcrumbs on top and pour a little goose fat over. Bake in oven for 20 minutes to brown topping and serve straight from dish.

Notes: An acceptable alternative is cold roast goose, with the fat which runs from it during cooking.

Preserved goose meat is very important for this dish and is a specialty of the Toulouse region in France.

If distilled water is used for soaking beans, they will tenderise in a shorter time — about 2 hours.

Serves 8

VEGETABLES
Les Légumes

ARTICHOKES remain a mystery vegetable, often overlooked in the market place for more common greens. Throughout Europe, the cookery technique involved has been passed from generation to generation and many beautiful recipes have evolved.

Read the following instructions and experiment with this interesting vegetable.

GLOBE ARTICHOKES WITH VARIOUS SAUCES
Artichauts aux sauces variées

6 medium-sized artichokes
juice 1 lemon
1½ cups either Hollandaise, Velouté,
  Mayonnaise or Remoulade Sauce (see
  recipe)

To cook artichokes whole, trim the stems off close to the bulbs. Using kitchen scissors, cut the pointed tips off the leaves in the bottom row. Lay artichokes on their sides and cut off the top few centimetres. Tie with string to prevent artichokes from opening during cooking.

Bring a saucepan of salted water to boil adding juice from a lemon. Add the artichokes and remove the pan from the heat. Cover and stand for 10 minutes, then drain.

Bring another saucepan salted water to boil and add artichokes. Boil until the leaves feel soft and are easily detached — approximately 25 minutes.

IF SERVING HOT
Drain the artichokes by standing them upside down. Carefully remove the top leaves by pulling. Pull out and discard the core. Replace leaves in centre. Place on a folded napkin with a sauceboat of the sauce of your choice.

The artichoke is eaten by plucking the leaves from the stem, dipping them in sauce and then popping the tender end in your mouth. The fibrous tip is not eaten so provide a side plate for these.

TO SERVE COLD
Drain and refresh under cold water. Turn upside down to drain and then serve.
Serves 6

FRENCH-FRIED ASPARAGUS SPEARS
Fritot d'asperges

1 bunch fresh asparagus
seasoned flour
1 egg beaten with ¼ cup milk
1 cup fresh breadcrumbs
oil for deep-frying
Tartare Sauce (see recipe)

Trim asparagus stems 2 cm from the base. Using a vegetable peeler, peel back any hard leaves on the stem.

Cook in boiling water until just tender. Drain and refresh under cold water. Drain thoroughly.

Gently toss asparagus in seasoned flour then dip in beaten egg and milk combination. Roll in breadcrumbs then press gently. Heat the oil and deep-fry the asparagus until golden brown. Drain on absorbent paper (paper towel).

Serve with a little Tartare Sauce.
Serves 2–4

ASPARAGUS WITH HOLLANDAISE SAUCE
Asperges à la Hollandaise

3 bunches asparagus
1 cup Hollandaise Sauce (see recipe)
fresh dill, to garnish

Trim asparagus so they are all the same length. Scrape off 'leaf' tips on the stem and tie in two bundles.

Bring a saucepan of salted water to the boil. Add asparagus and cook until tender — about 8 minutes.

Drain and serve hot with Hollandaise Sauce garnished with dill.
Serves 6

French-fried Asparagus Spears

Artichokes with various sauces

1 Cut pointed tips off artichoke leaves in bottom row

2 Tie with string to prevent artichokes from opening

Melt butter in same saucepan. Add onions, leeks, shallots and ham and cook over a low heat until tender but not browned.

Remove from heat and add flour, stirring until well blended. Return to heat and cook for one minute. Add garlic, reserved bean liquid and pinch of pepper. Stir until smooth then bring to boil, stirring. Reduce heat and simmer for 10 minutes. Add beans and simmer for a further 3 minutes.

Beat the egg yolk with vinegar, stir in 2–3 tablespoons of hot sauce, then add to the beans. Heat without boiling until thickened.

Serve garnished with parsley.
Serves 6

HARICOT BEANS WITH FRENCH BEANS
Haricots blanc et verts

500 g dried haricot beans
1 clove garlic, crushed (minced)
1 bouquet garni
salt to taste
500 g French beans, topped and tailed
75 g butter
3 tablespoons plain flour
3 cups Court Bouillon (see recipe)
freshly ground black pepper

Rinse the haricot beans and place into a large bowl. Cover with cold water and soak for several hours or overnight, changing the water twice.

Drain and rinse the haricot beans then place in a large saucepan with fresh water to cover. Add garlic and bouquet garni. Cover and bring to boil. Reduce heat and simmer covered for ¾–1 hour or until beans are tender. Season with salt halfway through the cooking time.

Cook the French beans separately in boiling water for 8 minutes until tender.

Drain and combine the beans, discarding bouquet garni and garlic.

Melt butter in a heavy-based saucepan, sprinkle in flour and cook, stirring for 1 minute, to obtain a smooth roux. Gradually add the stock, stirring constantly and bring to boil. Reduce heat and simmer for 5 minutes until sauce thickens, stirring occasionally. Add pepper to taste.

Stir the beans through the sauce and gently heat through. Transfer to a dish and serve.
Serves 6

French Beans with Ham, Mushrooms and Tomatoes

FRENCH BEANS WITH HAM, MUSHROOMS AND TOMATOES
Haricots verts à la Portugaise

1 kg French beans, topped and tailed
50 g butter
100 g ham, cut into strips
100 g mushrooms, sliced
4 tomatoes, skinned, seeded and chopped
salt and pepper
pinch garlic salt

Boil beans in salted water for 20 minutes and drain.

Heat butter in a frying pan. Sauté ham and mushrooms for 5 minutes. Add beans and tomatoes, salt, pepper and garlic salt.

Simmer for 6 minutes, stirring occasionally, then serve.
Serves 6

GREEN BEANS WITH HAM
Haricots verts au jambon

1 kg French beans, trimmed and strung
50 g butter
2 onions, finely chopped
2 leeks, washed and finely sliced
2 shallots (spring onions, scallions), finely sliced
250 g thickly sliced leg ham, diced
1 tablespoon flour
1 clove garlic, crushed (minced)
pinch freshly ground black pepper
1 × 60 g egg yolk
1 tablespoon white wine vinegar
2 tablespoons finely chopped parsley, to garnish

Bring a saucepan of salted water to boil. Add beans and cook for 5–6 minutes or until just tender. Drain, reserving 1 cup of liquid.

FRENCH-FRIED BRUSSELS SPROUTS
Choux de Bruxelles frites

400 g brussels sprouts
¼ cup flour seasoned with salt and pepper
1 egg beaten with 2 tablespoons milk
1 cup dried breadcrumbs
oil for deep-frying

Remove stem end from brussels sprouts and pull back any discoloured outer leaves. Bring a saucepan of salted water to the boil, add brussels sprouts and cook, uncovered, until just starting to tenderise. Drain well.

Place seasoned flour in a plastic bag. Add brussels sprouts, a few at a time, shaking to coat with flour.

Dip in beaten egg then roll in breadcrumbs. Deep-fry until golden brown and crisp, then serve with a sauce of your choice.
Serves 4

SAUTÉED CABBAGE WITH BACON
Chou au lard

150 g bacon, rind removed and chopped
2 tablespoons red wine vinegar
1 small cabbage, core removed and finely shredded
salt and freshly ground black pepper

Place bacon in a heavy-based saucepan and cook over a high heat until the fat starts to run and the bacon is crisp. Remove from heat, add vinegar, cabbage and seasonings. Return to heat and cook stirring constantly until well combined and the cabbage is tender.
Serves 6

BRAISED RED CABBAGE WITH APPLES
Chou rouge braisé aux pommes

30 g butter
1 large onion, sliced
1 red cabbage, cored and coarsely shredded
salt and freshly ground black pepper
200 mL Chicken Stock (see recipe)
pinch sugar
1 bay leaf
1 clove
3 Granny Smith apples, cored and thinly sliced

Melt butter in a large, heavy-based saucepan. Add onion and fry gently until tender and just starting to brown. Add cabbage and seasoning to taste. Moisten with half the stock. Stir in sugar, bay leaf and clove, then cover and simmer over a low heat until tender, about 45 minutes.

Add apples to the pan, stirring to combine. Cover and cook a further 20 minutes or until the apples are tender but still retaining their shape.

Remove and discard the bay leaf and clove, then taste to adjust seasoning. Serve immediately.
Serves 4–6

Braised Red Cabbage with Apples

RAISIN-GLAZED CARROTS
Carottes glacées aux raisins

500 g carrots, peeled and sliced
pinch salt
1 teaspoon dried rosemary
60 g butter
1 tablespoon brown sugar
¼ cup raisins, soaked
salt and pepper
1 tablespoon finely chopped parsley

Bring a saucepan of salted water to the boil. Add carrots and rosemary and cook until just tender — about 5 minutes.

Drain and return to saucepan with butter and brown sugar. Cook over medium heat, stirring occasionally until golden brown and glazed.

Drain the raisins, add to carrots with seasoning to taste and parsley. Serve immediately.
Serves 6

CAULIFLOWER WITH CHEESE SAUCE
Chou-fleur au gratin

lemon juice
1 bead cauliflower, trimmed and separated
    into florets
1 cup Béchamel Sauce (see recipe)
100 g Gruyère cheese, grated
60 g butter, diced
1 cup buttered fresh breadcrumbs

Preheat oven to 200°C (425°F).
Bring a saucepan of salted water to boil. Add a squeeze of lemon (this prevents discolouration) and the cauliflower.
Boil for 15 minutes or until quite tender. Scatter in the base of a well-greased ovenproof dish.
Pour the sauce evenly over the cauliflower then top with the cheese, cubes of butter and finally breadcrumbs. Bake in the upper part of the oven for 15 minutes or until golden brown.
Serves 6

CELERY IN RÉMOULADE SAUCE
Céleris rémoulade

1 small bead celery
½ cup Rémoulade Sauce (see recipe)

Remove the thicker outside stalks from the celery and reserve for stock or other recipes. Wash the remaining celery and cut diagonally into thin slices. Blanch in boiling water for 1 minute then drain and refresh under cold water. Drain thoroughly and place in a serving dish. Spoon over the sauce and serve cold.
Serves 6

CHICORY WITH LEMON JUICE
Endives au citron

4 chicory
60 g butter
1 tablespoon sugar
salt and freshly ground black pepper
juice of 1 lemon

Remove and discard any damaged outer leaves from the chicory. Wash well in cold water and cut a slit along the length of one side of each chicory.
Melt the butter in a large flameproof casserole dish. Arrange the chicory in a single layer over the base of the dish and sprinkle with sugar. Season with salt and

pepper to taste then sprinkle with lemon juice. Cover closely with a sheet of greaseproof (waxproof) paper and bake at 180°C (350°F) for 30 minutes or until tender.
Serve immediately from the casserole.
Serves 4

EGGPLANT AND TOMATO BAKE
Timbale d'aubergines aux tomates

For convenience, the pie can be prepared in advance and then baked when required.

1 kg small to medium-sized eggplants
    (aubergines), sliced
salt
seasoned flour
½ cup olive oil
220 g mozzarella cheese, sliced
¾ cup home-made Herbed Tomato Sauce
    (see recipe)
60 g freshly grated Parmesan cheese

Preheat oven to 180°C (350°F). Sprinkle eggplant with salt and leave for 30 minutes then rinse and drain thoroughly. Dust slices with seasoned flour. Heat ½ the oil in a frying pan and fry eggplant, in batches, until softened, adding more oil to pan if necessary. Drain eggplant on absorbent paper (paper towel).
Lightly grease a deep cake tin, about 18–20 cm in diameter. Make layers of eggplant, mozzarella and Tomato Sauce, starting with eggplant and finishing with Tomato Sauce, seasoning each layer with salt and pepper. Top with Parmesan cheese then bake for 20–30 minutes. Allow 2 minutes to cool. Cut into wedges and serve as an accompaniment to veal, lamb, beef or poultry dishes.
Serves 6–8

BRAISED FENNEL
Fenouil braisé

1 × 450 g bulb fennel, trimmed and
    quartered
1 carrot, chopped
1 onion, chopped
75 g bacon fat or ⅓ cup oil
1 chicken stock cube dissolved in 2 cups
    water
salt and pepper
SAUCE
25 g butter
¼ cup flour
2 tablespoons tomato paste

Preheat oven to 180°C (350°F).
Parboil fennel in salted water for 5 minutes and refresh. Lightly fry carrot and onion in bacon fat. Add drained fennel,

pour over chicken stock and transfer to an ovenproof dish. Season and braise, covered, for 1 hour in oven.
To make sauce, prepare a roux with butter and flour and stir in tomato paste. Pour over strained braising liquor. Bring to boil and season to taste. Simmer for 15 minutes and pour over fennel.
Serves 4

LEEKS VINAIGRETTE
Poireaux à la vinaigrette

500 g leeks, washed and cut in ½
½ cup water
VINAIGRETTE DRESSING
2 tablespoons olive oil
1 tablespoon cider vinegar
1 small onion, finely chopped
1 clove garlic, crushed (minced)
freshly ground black pepper
1 tablespoon chopped parsley, to garnish

Remove root end of leek. Place in a saucepan with water. Cover and cook over a low heat for 15 minutes. Drain and cool then place in a serving dish.
To make dressing: combine all the ingredients, mixing until well blended. Pour dressing over leeks and serve garnished with parsley.
Serves 4

LEEKS WITH EGG AND PARSLEY SAUCE
Poireaux à la paysanne

3 leeks, well-washed
2 eggs, hard-boiled
60 g unsalted butter
salt and freshly ground black pepper, to
    taste
2 tablespoons finely chopped parsley, to
    garnish

Bring a saucepan of salted water to boil.
Remove and discard leek roots. Slice in ½ lengthwise then in ½ again so that the leeks are approximately 12 cm long. Tie with string to form 2 bundles and drop into boiling water. Cook, uncovered for 25 minutes.
Peel the hard-boiled eggs and finely chop or mash. Melt the butter over a gentle heat and gradually add to the eggs, stirring constantly until well-blended. Season with salt and pepper to taste.
Strain the leeks and arrange on a serving platter removing the string. Spoon the egg sauce over the leeks and serve garnished with chopped parsley.
Serves 6

Leeks Vinaigrette

STUFFED MUSHROOMS
Champignons farcis

8 mushroom caps, wiped clean
30 g butter
1 slice white bread, crusts removed
2 tablespoons milk
1 tablespoon chopped parsley
1 small onion, finely chopped
1 clove garlic, crushed (minced)
salt and pepper
1 tablespoon oil
¼ cup white wine
2 tablespoons chopped parsley, to garnish

Remove stalks from mushrooms and finely chop. Melt butter in a frying pan and cook mushrooms for 5 minutes, turning once. Remove from pan and drain on absorbent paper (paper towel).

Soak bread in milk then squeeze out until almost dry. Combine with mushroom stems, parsley, onion, garlic, salt and pepper.

Place mushroom caps, dark side facing up, in a baking dish. Brush mushrooms with oil to prevent drying out. Spoon a little stuffing onto each one. Sprinkle over the wine, cover and bake at 180°C (350°F) for 20 minutes.

Garnish with chopped parsley.
Serves 4

HOT ONION SALAD
Oignons marinés

Hot or cold, the following recipe makes a wonderful accompaniment for grilled meat.

SAUCE
500 g tomatoes
2 onions, roughly chopped
3 cloves garlic, crushed (minced)
1 bouquet garni
salt and pepper
sprig basil
¼ cup olive oil

SALAD
1 kg small onions
100 g sultanas
1 cup white wine vinegar
½ cup olive oil
1 bouquet garni
salt and pepper
2–3 tablespoons sugar

Combine all the sauce ingredients and cook over medium heat for 30 minutes or until tender and pulpy. Pour into a sieve and rub with a wooden spoon to extract as much liquid as possible.

Peel onions and place in a large heavy-based saucepan. Add the sauce, remaining ingredients and just enough water to cover the onions. Bring to boil, stirring. Reduce heat and simmer, uncovered for 1 hour or until onions are tender.

Taste for seasoning, adding a little extra sugar to counteract the acidity.

Serve hot or allow to cool to appreciate the flavour further.
Serves 6

FRENCH PEAS
Petits pois à la Française

450 g small peas
225 g button onions, peeled
50 g shredded lettuce leaves
salt and pepper
1½ teaspoons sugar
1¼ cups water or stock
2 tablespoons flour
25 g butter

Place peas in a pan, add onions, lettuce, salt, pepper and sugar. Add water and cook gently for 10–15 minutes. Strain, reserving liquid. Keep peas warm.

Pour liquid into a pan. Blend flour and butter together and add this mixture to liquid. Cook until thickened and add to peas. Mix well and serve.
Serves 4

LITTLE PEAS
Petits pois

400 g peas, fresh or frozen and thawed
4 small onions, peeled
3 lettuce leaves, shredded
salt and pepper
40 g butter
1 teaspoon butter
½ cup water

Place peas in a sieve and rinse with cold water. Combine all the ingredients in a saucepan, cover and quickly bring to boil. Remove lid and continue cooking until tender. Drain if necessary and serve.
Serves 4

POTATOES BOULANGÈRE
Pommes de terre à la boulangère

1¼ cups water
1 chicken stock cube
100 g butter
1 kg potatoes, peeled and thinly sliced
225 g onions, thinly sliced
salt and pepper
1 tablespoon chopped parsley, to garnish

Preheat oven to 200°C (400°F).
Boil water and crumble in stock cube.
Grease an ovenproof dish with 50 g butter. Arrange potatoes and onions in the dish, overlapping each other. Season, cover with stock and dot the top with remaining butter.

Bake in oven for 25 minutes, then reduce heat to 180°C (350°F). Cook for a further 20 minutes until potatoes have browned and absorbed all liquid.

Sprinkle with chopped parsley and serve with roast lamb or lamb chops.
Serves 4

DUCHESS POTATOES
Pommes de terre duchesse

potatoes
egg yolk
butter

Wash, peel and re-wash potatoes. Cut to an even size. Cook in salted water. Drain off water, place lid on saucepan and return to a low heat to dry out potatoes. Mash potatoes well to avoid any lumps. Add one egg yolk per 500 g potato. Stir vigorously. Mix in 30 g butter. Correct seasonings.

DAUPHINOIS POTATOES
Gratin de pommes de terre à la dauphinoise

1 kg potatoes
1 clove garlic, crushed (minced)
100 g butter, softened
2 eggs
2½ cups milk
¾ cup cream
salt and pepper
grated nutmeg
1 cup grated Gruyère cheese

Preheat oven to 200°C (400°F).
Peel potatoes, place in a saucepan of salted water and bring to boil. Boil for 1 minute, then drain, cool slightly and thinly slice.

Rub garlic around the inside of an ovenproof dish. Use 50 g butter to grease the dish.

Break eggs into a bowl, add milk, cream, salt, pepper and nutmeg and beat. Stir in ½ cup grated cheese.

Cover bottom of greased dish with a layer of potato slices. Cover with a little of the cream and cheese mixture. Continue with alternate layers of potato and cheese mixture until both are all used. Sprinkle top with remaining grated cheese and dot with butter.

Bake in oven for 45 minutes. Cover with foil if it becomes too brown. Serve with roast meat or grilled steak.
Note: For delicious variations, try adding layers of sautéed, sliced mushrooms and chopped onions. Never use raw potatoes in this dish — very often they will cause the milk to curdle. Parboiling the potatoes first or thickening the milk with cornflour (cornstarch) will prevent this.
Serves 4

Hot Onion Salad

74

RATATOUILLE

The flavour will develop and improve on keeping. Prepare and store in the refrigerator overnight.

3 medium-sized eggplants (aubergines),
  sliced 1 cm thick
salt and pepper, to taste
½ cup olive oil
3 onions, finely sliced
3–4 cloves garlic, crushed (minced)
500 g zucchini (courgettes), sliced
  diagonally
3 green capsicums (peppers), cored, seeded
  and sliced
500 g tomatoes, sliced thickly

Sprinkle eggplant slices with salt and leave for 30 minutes. Rinse and pat dry.

Heat half the oil in a heavy-based saucepan, add onions and garlic and cook until onion is soft. Add eggplant and zucchini and fry, in batches, for three minutes each side, adding extra oil if necessary. Return fried eggplant to pan and season with pepper. Add capsicum and tomatoes and season with more pepper. Cover pan and simmer for 45 minutes – 1 hour or until ratatouille is very soft.

Serve warm or chilled as an accompaniment to poached eggs, grilled or barbecued meats and poultry or with lentil dishes.
Serves 8

SPINACH WITH CREAM
Épinards à la crème

400 g English spinach, stalks removed
salt and pepper
½ cup Béchamel Sauce (see recipe)
3 tablespoons cream

Wash spinach well to remove grit.

Bring a saucepan of water to boil. Add spinach and cook for 5 minutes, uncovered. Drain and squeeze out excess moisture.

Chop finely and return to saucepan with seasoning to taste. Add Béchamel Sauce, stirring to combine. Add the cream and heat until starting to boil then serve.
Serves 4

GRILLED TOMATOES WITH BASIL BUTTER
Tomates grillés au beurre de basilic

Basil Butter can be frozen successfully. Keep some handy for barbecued meats, herb bread or baked potatoes.

6 tomatoes
oil
salt and pepper, to taste

BASIL BUTTER
90 g butter
1 clove garlic, crushed (minced)
2 tablespoons chopped basil or 1 tablespoon
  dried basil
1 tablespoon chopped parsley
good squeeze lemon juice

Beat butter until soft. Add remaining ingredients and season to taste with salt and pepper. Stir well until the ingredients are well-blended. Turn the butter onto a piece of foil into a log shape. Seal well and freeze until firm.

Van-dyke tomatoes. Preheat grill and lightly brush tomatoes with oil. Place tomatoes, cut side down, on grill tray and grill for 3–5 minutes. Turn, season with salt and pepper and grill for a further 3–5 minutes.

Cut Basil Butter into 12 slices. Place one slice on each tomato and serve hot as an accompaniment to scrambled eggs, grilled sausages or lamb chops.
Serves 6

SAVOURY-FILLED TOMATOES
Tomates farcies

Firm, round tomatoes make colourful containers for a variety of fillings. They can be served on their own as a first course or snack, or arranged on a serving platter for a decorative touch to the dinner table.

12 medium-sized tomatoes
2 cups cream cheese
½ green capsicum (pepper), seeded and very
  finely chopped
¼ teaspoon very finely chopped basil or
  pinch dried basil
salt and pepper to taste

Halve tomatoes and scoop out seeds and membranes with a teaspoon. Invert them onto a tray to drain while preparing filling. Pat tomato shells dry with absorbent paper (paper towels) before filling.

Mix all ingredients together thoroughly, season and spoon into tomato shells.
Serves 6

TRUFFLES are round black fungi which grow a few centimetres underground. They are found in only a few regions in France for about 2 months of the year and are therefore quite expensive. Limited amounts are sold fresh but the canned truffles are readily available from exclusive gourmet stores.

To enhance the flavour, add 2 tablespoons Madeira to the opened can of truffles and leave for 30 minutes. Keep the canned juice and use in sauces. Place truffles flat on the work bench and cut with a very sharp knife into small slivers. Use in omelettes, pâtés, stuffings or as garnish for canapés.

TRUFFLES WITH BUTTER SAUCE
Truffes à la crème

50 g canned truffles
130 g unsalted butter
¼ cup liquid from can of truffles
½ cup cream
salt and freshly ground black pepper
1 teaspoon lemon juice

Slice truffles into fine shreds.

Melt a small knob of butter in a saucepan. Add truffles and cook for 2 minutes. Add truffle liquid and cream. Season with salt and pepper, bring to boil and cook until liquid has reduced by ½. Add remaining butter a little at a time, stirring until well-blended. Add lemon juice then serve immediately.
Serves 2–4

WITLOF WITH HAM
Gratin d'endives

4 heads witlof (Belgian endive)
1 teaspoon sugar
salt and pepper
8 slices double smoked ham
2 cups Béchamel Sauce (see recipe)
50 g Gruyère cheese, grated

Blanch witlof in boiling salted water for 3–4 minutes. Drain, cool and cut in ½ removing the stem. Sprinkle with sugar, salt and pepper and wrap each ½ in a slice of ham.

Grease an ovenproof dish liberally with butter and arrange witlof in the base. Pour over Béchamel Sauce and sprinkle cheese on top.

Bake at 200°C (400°F) for 15–20 minutes or until golden brown. Serve as an entrée or an accompaniment to roast meat.
Serves 4

ZUCCHINI WITH CREAM SAUCE
Courgettes à la crème

1 kg zucchini (courgettes)
salt
30 g butter
1 tablespoon olive oil
2 shallots (spring onions, scallions), finely chopped
pepper, to taste
2 cups Crème Fraîche (see recipe) or thickened (double) cream.

Trim and grate zucchini. Sprinkle with salt and leave aside for 15 minutes. Squeeze the excess liquid from zucchini.

Combine the butter and oil in a frying pan and heat gently. Add the shallots and cook for 3 minutes or until tender. Increase the heat adding the zucchini. Stir and toss zucchini in pan until tender and all liquid has evaporated.

Add cream and simmer until thickened. Taste for seasoning and serve.
Serves 4–6

SAUTÉED ZUCCHINI WITH PARSLEY AND GARLIC BUTTER
Courgettes sautées au beurre d'ail

1 kg zucchini (courgettes)
60 g butter
1 clove garlic, crushed (minced)
2 tablespoons finely chopped parsley
salt and pepper, to taste

Wash zucchini and slice into 2 cm slices.

Melt butter in a large saucepan. When foaming add garlic and parsley. Cook for 2 minutes then add zucchini. Cover pan and shake to coat the zucchini liberally with butter. Season with salt and pepper and cook over a very low heat for 10 minutes or until tender.
Serves 4–6

COLD BUFFET
Préparations Froides

MUSHROOMS À LA GRECQUE
Champignons à la Grecque

3 tablespoons olive oil
3 onions, finely chopped
2 cloves garlic, bruised
¼ cup dry white wine
salt and pepper, to taste
bouquet garni
500 g mushrooms, wiped and trimmed
1 × 425 g can tomatoes, drained
chopped parsley, to garnish

Heat oil and cook onions and garlic until onions are golden brown. As garlic browns, remove and discard. Remove from the heat, slowly pour in wine, salt and pepper to taste and bouquet garni. Bring to boil, reduce heat and simmer for 5 minutes.

Add mushrooms and tomatoes, bring to boil, reduce heat and simmer for 20 minutes. Taste and adjust seasoning if necessary. Serve sprinkled with parsley.
Serves 6–8

CRUDITÉS

A colourful selection of raw vegetables will make a welcome change when served with dressings and sauces. The choice of vegetables should include a variety of colour and flavour.

100 g cherry tomatoes
2 sticks celery, diagonally sliced
100 g button mushrooms, wiped
6 baby carrots, peeled
100 g snow peas (mangetout), stalks removed
1 cucumber, peeled and sliced
1 each red and green capsicum (pepper), seeded and sliced into rings
200 g French beans, topped and tailed
1 cup Mayonnaise or Ravigote Sauce (see recipes)

Arrange the prepared vegetables attractively on a serving plate with a bowl of sauce of your choice in the centre.

Serve as soon as practicable as the vegetables will dry out and lose their crispness.
Serves 6

SMOKED EEL SALAD
Salade d'anguille fumée

250 g smoked eel, cut into pieces
250 g potatoes, cooked, peeled and diced
2 heads Belgian endive (witlof)
1 tablespoon chives, chopped
6 radishes, sliced
walnut halves, to garnish

DRESSING
juice and grated rind 1 large lemon
100 mL sour (dairy sour) cream
Tabasco sauce, to taste
1–2 tablespoons grated horseradish

Prepare dressing first. Combine all ingredients. Taste and adjust seasoning and chill until ready to use.

Remove skin from eel and slice meat off the bone in bite-sized pieces. Place eel, potatoes, endive, chives and radishes in a bowl. Pour over dressing and toss lightly but thoroughly. Serve garnished with walnuts.

Variation
If smoked eel is unavailable from your delicatessen, substitute smoked trout garnished with a little smoked salmon and sprays of dill.
Serves 4

OCTOPUS SALAD
Salade de poulpes

12 small octopi
1½ cups oil
1½ cups red wine
1 cup water
100 g carrots, in fine julienne
2 sticks celery, in fine julienne
100 g zucchini (courgettes), in fine julienne
1 leek, well-washed, in fine julienne
1 radicchio lettuce
1 mignonette lettuce
2 teaspoons pink peppercorns, drained, to garnish

DRESSING
1½ tablespoons red wine vinegar
3 tablespoons olive oil
1 clove garlic, crushed (minced)
¼ teaspoon sugar
salt

Wash octopi and cut off heads just below the eyes. Discard heads. Combine oil, red wine and water and bring to boil. Add octopi and simmer for 20–25 minutes or until tender. Drain, cook and cut into bite-sized pieces.

Line a salad platter with lettuce leaves and arrange vegetables and octopi pieces attractively on lettuce.

Combine dressing ingredients and pour over salad. Sprinkle with peppercorns.
Serves 4

ROAST BEEF SALAD
Boeuf Niçoise

60 g butter
750 g eye fillet, trimmed of sinew
freshly ground black pepper
2 mignonette lettuces
4 tomatoes, cut into quarters
45 g can anchovies, drained
1 green capsicum (pepper), seeded and sliced
1 cucumber, peeled, seeded and sliced
6 shallots (spring onions, scallions), diagonally sliced
3 sticks celery, diagonally sliced
4 hard-boiled eggs, shelled and halved
1 cup small black olives
1 cup Oil and Vinegar Dressing (see recipe)

Preheat oven to 200°C (400°F)

Heat butter in a baking pan over moderately high heat. Add beef and quickly roll in butter to brown meat on all sides. Season well with black pepper.

Bake for 20 minutes in preheated oven. Lift meat from pan and wrap in foil. Set aside until cool, then carve into fine slivers.

Wash lettuce and divide into leaves. Line a large salad bowl with lettuce. Arrange remaining salad ingredients and beef on top of lettuce. Pour dressing over salad just before serving.
Serves 6

From bottom right-hand corner, clockwise: Roast Beef Salad, Mushrooms à la Greque, Cheese Straws, Octopus Salad, Smoked Trout Pâté, Rabbit and Prune Terrine

SCALLOP TERRINE
Terrine de coquilles St Jacques

500 g scallops
200 g John Dory or sole fillets, skinned
2 tablespoons finely chopped shallots
  (spring onions, scallions)
2 eggs
salt and pepper, to taste
1 tablespoon flour
100 mL sour (dairy sour) cream
1 egg (extra)
100 mL thickened (double) cream

Rinse scallops and drain well. Cut orange roes from white of scallops and set aside.

Combine white of scallops, fillets, shallots, eggs, seasonings and flour in a food processor and process until finely minced. Chill for 1 hour.

Process chilled mixture for 1 minute. Add sour cream and process until light and fluffy. Transfer ¾ of this mixture to a bowl and set aside.

Add orange roes to remaining mixture together with egg and thickened cream. Process until well-combined.

Lightly grease a 6 cup loaf dish and line with greaseproof (waxproof) paper. Spread ½ white scallop mixture into base of dish, top with roe layer and finish with remaining white scallop mixture.

Cover loaf dish with greased greaseproof (waxproof) paper. Bake in a water bath at 130°C (300°F) for 40 minutes or until centre of terrine feels slightly 'springy' to touch.

Serves 6

SMOKED TROUT PÂTÉ
Pâté de truite fumee

3 medium-sized smoked trout
60 g butter, softened
3 slices white bread, crusts removed
¼ cup milk
150 g cream cheese
½ teaspoon anchovy essence
juice ½ lemon
salt and ground black pepper

Remove head, skin and all bones from trout and purée flesh in a food processor or blender. Gradually add butter and blend well.

Soak bread in milk for 5 minutes, then squeeze out excess milk and add this and all remaining ingredients to puréed fish, blending constantly. Spoon mixture into well-oiled mould (approximately 2 cup capacity). Refrigerate overnight. Unmould pâté and serve.

Serve 6–8

Left to right: Scallop Terrine, Smoked Trout Pâté and Chicken Liver Pâté

CHICKEN LIVER PÂTÉ
Pâté de foie

500 g chicken livers
250 g calf's liver
5 g butter
1 fatty pork chop
1 onion, chopped
2 cloves garlic, chopped
1 egg, beaten
¾ cup cream
⅓ cup flour
1 teaspoon salt
ground black pepper
1 teaspoon chopped thyme
1 teaspoon chopped basil
2 tablespoons brandy
3 rashers bacon

Clean chicken livers and purée using a food processor or blender. Trim calf's liver and quickly fry in hot butter for a few minutes and then cut up and purée. Remove fat from chop and cut up meat. Combine meats with all ingredients except bacon.

Line a 5–6 cup pâté mould or loaf dish with trimmed bacon and spoon in pâté mixture. Cover with lid or foil. Place in baking dish containing sufficient water to come halfway up mould and bake at 160°C (325°F). Cook for 45 minutes. Remove cover and cook another 15 minutes. Cover and refrigerate for 24 hours before serving. This pâté can be refrigerated for up to 1 week.

Serves 12

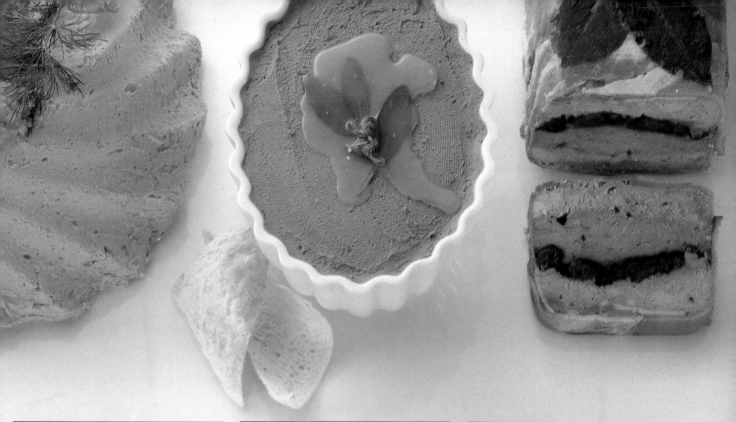

SALMON CREAM MOUSSE
Mousseline de saumon

2 × 220 g cans red salmon, drained
1 teaspoon Dijon-style mustard
½ cup white wine vinegar
1 tablespoon gelatine
¼ cup water
1 tablespoon horseradish cream
⅓ cup Mayonnaise (see recipe)
½ cup celery, finely chopped
1 tablespoon capers, drained and finely chopped
60 g shallots (spring onions, scallions), finely chopped
3 tablespoons pickled cucumber, drained and finely chopped
¼ cup cream, whipped

Drain salmon and remove any hard bones. Place salmon in a food processor or blender with mustard and white wine vinegar and process until smooth.

Mix gelatine with water and dissolve over hot water before combining with horseradish cream, Mayonnaise and dissolved gelatine. Stir into salmon mixture and add celery, capers, shallots and cucumber. Lastly, fold in the cream.

Pour into a lightly oiled 1 litre capacity mould and cover with lightly oiled greaseproof (waxproof) paper and chill overnight or until set. To unmould the mousse, dip mould into warm water for 5 seconds and turn upside down onto a serving platter decorated with a choice of garnishes.
Serves 6–8

QUICK CHICKEN LIVER PÂTÉ
Pâté de foie de volaille

125 g butter
1 small onion, finely chopped
1 clove garlic, crushed (minced)
200 g chicken livers, cleaned
1 sprig thyme
1 tablespoon brandy
salt and pepper, to taste

Melt 25 g butter in a pan and gently fry the onions until tender, about 5 minutes. Add the garlic and cook a further 2 minutes.

Add liver and thyme to pan and cook, turning constantly for 5 minutes. Remove pan from heat and cool slightly. Place the mixture in a sieve and rub to form a smooth purée or process in a blender.

Add 75 g of the remaining butter and beat until smooth. Add brandy and seasoning to taste.

Spoon the pâté into a serving dish or individual pâté pots smoothing the top with a spatula. Melt remaining butter in a pan and pour over the pâté. Refrigerate until set.
Serves 4

Left to right: Salmon Cream Mousse, Quick Chicken Liver Pâté and Rabbit and Prune Terrine

RABBIT AND PRUNE TERRINE
Terrine de lapin aux pruneaux

180 g prunes
red wine
1 kg rabbit legs or 2 kg whole rabbit
500 g belly of pork
250 g stewing veal
375 g bacon rashers, rind removed
3–4 dried juniper berries, soaked overnight
1 teaspoon dried sage
1 teaspoon dried oregano
1 teaspoon ground mace

MARINADE
juice 1 orange
3 tablespoons brandy
10 dried juniper berries, crushed (minced)
10 whole allspice, crushed (minced)
8 black peppercorns, crushed (minced)
4 bay leaves
1 teaspoon salt

Soak prunes overnight in red wine sufficient to cover all the prunes.

Remove flesh from rabbit and cut into small pieces. Arrange in shallow dish and then combine all marinade ingredients and pour over rabbit. Cover and refrigerate 8 hours or overnight, turning occasionally.

Remove and discard rind from pork and mince pork with veal in food processor or blender.

Grease a 1 litre earthenware dish and with the bay leaves taken from marinade, arrange these on bottom of dish to form a pattern with juniper berries. Lay all but 2 rashers of bacon on bottom and sides of dish. *continued page 82*

Drain rabbit, reserving marinade and put a layer of rabbit over bacon. Follow with sprinkling of herbs, a few prunes, a layer of pork and veal, and so on until all ingredients are used up. Strain marinade and pour over terrine. Lay 2 bay leaves on top and cover with remaining bacon.

Cover with greased foil and a lid. Put dish in a pan of water and bake at 160°C (320°F) for 1½–2 hours until a skewer inserted in the centre comes out clean. Stand for 30 minutes. Weight down terrine and leave for several hours or overnight.

To serve, dip terrine quickly in very hot water and turn out onto serving dish.
Serves 10–14

MACKEREL IN SPICY CITRUS MARINADE
Filets de maquereau vinaigrette au citron

6 medium-sized pieces of Spanish mackerel cutlets or fillets or mullet fillets
4 tablespoons seasoned flour
¼ cup olive oil for frying
100 mL lime or lemon juice
100 mL white wine vinegar
100 mL orange juice
200 mL water
⅓ cup olive oil
2 bay leaves
8 whole peppercorns
1 chilli, seeded and finely chopped
1 capsicum (pepper), finely shredded
1 onion, finely shredded
zest 1 orange, finely shredded

Dust fillets lightly with flour. Heat oil to 190°C (375°F). Fry fillets until they just flake when tested. Do not overcook or fillets become tough when cooled. Drain on absorbent paper (paper towel) and place in a shallow glass or ceramic dish.

Combine all remaining ingredients in a saucepan and simmer for 5 minutes. Pour marinade over fish, cool to room temperature, cover with foil and refrigerate overnight.

Drain off excess liquid and serve on a large platter.
Serves 6

PRESERVED GOOSE
Confit d'oie

4 kg goose, oven-ready
450 g mixed goose fat
PICKLING MIXTURE
1 cup coarse salt
¼ cup sugar
pinch fresh thyme
1 bay leaf
½ teaspoon mixed spice and ground mace
good pinch pepper

Cut up goose into 8 portions, cutting the 2 legs in half at the knee joints. Carve the 2 wings at the base of wishbone, between shoulder bone and the first part of winglets. Cut breast into 2 portions. Prick goose pieces all over with a fork.

To make pickling mixture: blend all pickling ingredients together. Place goose pieces in a 7.5 cm deep earthenware dish, large enough to hold all pieces, and sprinkle with pickling mixture. Place in refrigerator for 24–36 hours.

Remove dish of goose pieces from refrigerator, brush off pickling mixture and wipe pieces clean.

In a large saucepan, heat mixture of goose fat and lard to 100°C (210°F). Add goose pieces to fat, a few at a time, making sure they are completely immersed. Reduce heat and simmer very gently for 2 hours (the goose must not fry but just boil, so do not allow fat to become too hot). Repeat this process until all pieces are cooked.

Remove goose pieces; strain and reserve fat. Discard ribs and backbones from goose meat, leaving leg and wing bones. Place pieces in a clean earthenware dish. If not needed immediately, pour some clean strained fat over them, cover with aluminium foil when cold, and store in refrigerator.
Note: Chicken fat can be used instead of goose fat but should be mixed with an equal quantity of lard.
Serves 8

BREADCASES FILLED WITH HERBED SNAILS IN RED WINE
Croustades à l'escargot

1 loaf unsliced white bread, crusts removed
90 g Clarified Butter (see recipe)
30 g butter
60 g shallots (spring onions, scallions), finely chopped
1 clove garlic, crushed (minced)
½ cup red wine
1 bay leaf
½ teaspoon finely chopped thyme
1 teaspoon finely chopped parsley
ground black pepper
1 × 125 g can snails, drained and finely chopped
1 teaspoon cornflour (cornstarch)
1 tablespoon water

Cut bread into 2.5 cm cubes and form a deep indentation in each cube with your thumb. Brush cubes with Clarified Butter and bake at 170°C (325°F) for 20 minutes or until golden. Keep breadcases warm.

Heat butter and fry shallots and garlic for 2 minutes. Add red wine, herbs and seasonings and simmer until reduced by ½. Add snails and heat through. Thicken mixture with the cornflour combined with water. Remove bay leaf. Divide snail mixture between the breadcases and serve immediately.
Makes approximately 24 hors d'oeuvre

CHEESE STRAWS
Pailletes au fromage

250 g puff pastry, home-made or pre-packaged and thawed
⅓ cup grated Parmesan cheese
½ cup Leicester or other hard cheese, grated
pinch cayenne
pinch paprika

Roll out pastry to a rectangle about 3 mm thick and mix grated cheese with paprika and cayenne and sprinkle over pastry. Fold in ½ and roll out again to same thickness.

Preheat oven to 200°C (400°F).

Roll out pastry to the width of baking tray and cut into strips 1 cm wide. Place on a board and twist with both hands, then place on a greased baking tray.

Bake for 8 minutes or until golden in colour.

Cut the strips in regular lengths of 10 cm.
Makes about 32 straws

Assorted canapés

CHEESE CANAPÉS

125 g Roquefort cheese
125 g cream cheese
salt and pepper
12 slices bread
2 eggs, hard-boiled, shelled and chopped
1 tablespoon chopped parsley

Cream together the two cheeses until smooth, adding salt and pepper.

Cut bread into 24 shapes using an oval metal cutter, spread each oval with cheese and top with a little chopped egg. Garnish with a sprinkle of parsley.

PAPRIKA CANAPÉS

125 g cream cheese, softened
1 tablespoon onion, finely grated
2 teaspoons ground paprika
salt and pepper
8 thick slices brown bread
paprika, to serve

Beat cream cheese until soft and smooth. Gradually add onion, paprika, salt and pepper and beat until combined.

Remove crusts from the bread and cut into diamond shapes approximately 5 cm long and 3 cm wide. Spread thickly with cream cheese mixture, sprinkle canapés with a little paprika and serve.

AVOCADO CANAPÉS

1 ripe avocado, seeded, peeled and mashed
125 g cream cheese, softened
juice ½ lemon
1 teaspoon Dijon mustard
salt and pepper
12 slices bread cut into 4 cm rounds
2 eggs, hard-boiled, shelled and sliced
1 tablespoon chopped parsley

Combine avocado, cream cheese, lemon juice, mustard, salt and pepper and mix to form a smooth paste.

Top each round of bread with a slice of egg, a little parsley and some of the avocado mixture. Serve immediately.

PRAWN CANAPÉS

125 g cream cheese, softened
125 g butter, softened
pinch salt
1 teaspoon horseradish cream
12 slices white or brown bread
400 g peeled small prawns
2 tablespoons capers, chopped

Beat together cream cheese and butter and season with salt and horseradish cream.

Using a 4 cm fluted metal cutter, cut 2 rounds from each slice of bread. Spread bread evenly with cream cheese mixture.

Arrange prawns on top of the rounds and decorate with chopped capers.

DESSERTS AND CAKES
Entrements et Gâteaux

Pastry

SHORTCRUST PASTRY
Pâte brisée

2½ cups flour
pinch salt
1 teaspoon sugar
200 g chilled butter, diced small
1 egg yolk
1 tablespoon iced water
few drops lemon juice

Sift together flour, salt and sugar. Rub in butter, using tips of fingers until mixture resembles fine breadcrumbs. Whisk together egg yolk, iced water and lemon juice. Blend into flour mixing with a round-bladed knife to form a pliable ball. Do not add all the liquid at once as mixture may not require all. Do not overmix dough. Wrap and refrigerate for at least 1 hour. Roll out the dough on a floured board or between 2 sheets greaseproof (waxproof) paper. Use as required.

Variation
Sweet Shortcrust Pastry is made exactly like a normal shortcrust except that sugar is mixed into the flour before you begin. For the above quantity, add 2 tablespoons caster sugar.
Makes sufficient dough to line 2 × 20 cm flan tins.

CHOUX PASTRY
Pâté à choux

⅔ cup flour
⅔ cup water
pinch salt
75 g butter
3–4 eggs, slightly beaten

Sift flour onto a piece of greaseproof (waxproof) paper. In a saucepan heat water, salt and butter until butter is melted. Remove pan from heat and add all flour at once. Beat vigorously with a wooden spoon until mixture is smooth. Return pan to low heat and beat until mixture pulls away from sides of pan to form a ball. Cool to tepid.

Beat in eggs, a little at a time, beating well between each addition. The mixture should be glossy and hold its shape when dropped from the spoon. Use as required. *Note:* All the egg may not be needed. The mixture will not hold its shape if too much egg is added.
Makes sufficient dough to line 1 × 20 cm flan tin

SWEET FLAN PASTRY
Pâté sucree

Pâte Sucrée is fine and delicate and will remain crisp when filled with fruits or custard.

1 cup flour
pinch salt
60 g butter, softened
⅓ cup caster sugar
2 egg yolks
2 drops vanilla

Sift flour and salt onto a work surface or marble slab making a well in the centre. Place remaining ingredients in the well and pinch them together using the fingertips.
Gradually incorporate all the flour and mix to form a smooth dough.
Knead on a lightly floured surface for 1–2 minutes. Wrap in plastic wrap and chill for 1 hour before using. Chill again after rolling and shaping. Roll between 2 sheets of freezer plastic wrap or on a lightly floured board.
Use as required.
Makes sufficient dough to line 1 × 20 cm flan tin.

Sweets

STRAWBERRY FLAN
Tarte aux fraises

1 quantity Sweet Shortcrust Pastry (see recipe)
1 egg yolk
250 g stawberries
1 tablespoon redcurrant jam or jelly

GLAZE
2 tablespoons redcurrant or strawberry jam
2 tablespoons sugar
2 tablespoons water
1½ tablespoons cornflour (cornstarch)

Preheat oven to 190°C (375°F).
On a lightly floured board roll out dough 5 mm thick. Lift onto rolling pin and line base and sides of a 20 cm flan tin and place on a greased baking tray. Cut off extra pastry.
Prick flan all over with a fork. Line with greaseproof (waxproof) paper and rice and bake blind for 20 minutes.
Remove paper and rice. Brush sides with beaten egg yolk and return to oven for 5 minutes until a deep golden colour. Allow to cool.
Spread base with redcurrant jam. Gently rinse strawberries and drain on absorbent paper (paper towel). Starting from the middle of the flan, arrange strawberries in concentric circles.
To make glaze: boil jam, sugar and water in a saucepan. Mix cornflour with a little water and add to pan. Stir for 2 minutes until glaze clears. While it is hot, brush it on flan. If using strawberry jam, strain before pouring. Allow to cool.
Serves 8

Strawberry Flan and Apple Flan

APPLE FLAN
Tarte aux pommes

1 quantity Sweet Shortcrust Pastry (see recipe)
350 g Golden Delicious apples, peeled, cored and thinly sliced
juice ½ lemon
1 tablespoon sugar

GLAZE
2 tablespoons apricot jam
1 tablespoon water
1 teaspoon cornflour (cornstarch)
1 tablespoon water

Preheat oven to 200°C (400°F).

Roll out pastry to line base and sides of a 23 cm flan tin. Bake blind for 10 minutes.

Arrange apple slices in overlapping rows in flan shell. Brush with lemon juice, sprinkle with sugar and bake in oven for 15 minutes, until golden brown.

Melt jam in 100 mL water. Mix cornflour with 1 tablespoon water and add to the jam. Boil glaze 3–4 minutes until glossy. Pour glaze over apples and serve. The flan may also be served cold.

Serves 4–6

CARAMELISED APPLE TART
Tarte tatin

1 quantity Sweet Shortcrust Pastry (see recipe)

FILLING
1 kg sweet dessert apples, peeled, cored and sliced
75 g butter
⅔ cup caster sugar

Preheat oven to 200°C (400°F).

Grease a 20 cm flan tin with half the butter and sprinkle with half the sugar. Arrange apple slices over, then sprinkle with remaining sugar and dot with remaining butter.

Roll out pastry dough thinly on a lightly floured board and cut a neat circle a little larger than flan tin. Place circle over apples, tucking the edge inside flan tin and bake for 25–30 minutes until dough is cooked and apples have caramelised.

Invert tart onto a serving plate and serve warm.

Serves 6

PEAR TART
Tarte aux poires

1 quantity of Pâte Sucrée (see recipe) or 2 sheets ready-rolled shortcrust pastry
4 pears, peeled, cored and halved

SYRUP
2 cups water
1 cup sugar
strip of lemon rind

FRANGIPANI CREAM
210 g unsalted butter
½ cup sugar
2 large eggs, beaten
1 cup blanched almonds, ground
1 tablespoon flour
almond liqueur or kirsch or almond essence

GLAZE
¼ cup apricot jam, warmed and sieved
whipped cream, to serve
almond liqueur or cinnamon

Line base and sides of a 20 cm metal flan tin with Pâte Sucrée or ready-rolled pastry. Trim edges and bake blind at 200°C (400°F) for 10 minutes. Cool before filling.

Cook pears in water, sugar and lemon rind, until just tender. Cool in syrup then drain on absorbent paper (paper towel).

Cream butter and sugar together and add eggs a little at a time, beating well. Add almonds, flour and kirsch.

Spoon ½ the Frangipani Cream over pastry base. Arrange pear halves on this, cut side facing down. Spread remaining cream mixture around and over the pears. Bake at 180°C (350°F) for 40 minutes, until cream is set and golden brown. Brush with apricot glaze. Serve with whipped cream very lightly flavoured with almond liqueur or cinnamon.

Serves 6

PROFITEROLES AND CHOCOLATE RUM SAUCE
Profiteroles au chocolat et rhum

500 g Choux Pastry (see recipe)
1¼ cups thickened (double) cream, whipped
1 tablespoon caster sugar

SAUCE
250 g plain chocolate
¼ cup rum
1 tablespoon caster sugar
25 g butter

Preheat oven to 200°C (400°F).

On a greased baking sheet, put 18 heaped teaspoons of Choux Pastry, well separated.

Bake for 20 minutes until well risen and golden brown. Remove from oven, make a small slit in each to allow steam to escape. Return to oven for 5 minutes to dry out, then cool.

Just before serving, whip the cream with sugar until stiff. Using a piping bag, fill each profiterole through side slit and pile them on a dish.

To make sauce: melt chocolate and rum in a bowl over a saucepan of boiling water. Add sugar and butter and mix well. Pour over profiteroles and serve cold.

Makes 18

CROQUEMBOUCHE

1 quantity Choux Pastry (see recipe)

To make a tall Croquembouche you will need a Croquembouche cone. This adds support and helps the dessert to keep for hours. The cones are available from kitchenware stores.

FILLING
3 cups thickened (double) cream
½ cup icing sugar
2 tablespoons Grand Marnier
2 teaspoons grated orange rind
2 quantities Spun Sugar (see recipe)

Drop slightly rounded teaspoons of choux mixture onto a greased baking tray about 5 cm apart. Bake at 200°C (400°F) for 10 minutes. Reduce temperature to 180°C (350°F) and bake a further 15–20 minutes or until well puffed and golden brown.

Remove from oven, make a small slit in the side of each puff to allow steam to escape. Return puffs to oven for a few minutes to dry out and cool completely. Repeat with remaining pastry until all is finished.

Make a small hole in the base of each puff and pipe in a little filling.

Place Croquembouche cone on a plate. Dip each puff into caramel mixture for Spun Sugar and arrange the cone, joining the puffs together as you go.

Decorate Croquembouche with remaining Spun Sugar.

Serve within 6 hours or the puffs will soften.

To make filling: whip cream and icing sugar together to form soft peaks. Fold in Grand Marnier and orange rind.

Serves 6

Croquembouche

SPUN SUGAR

1 cup caster sugar
pinch cream of tartar
½ cup water

Combine all ingredients in a small saucepan and heat gently stirring until the sugar dissolves. Using a wet pastry brush, brush away any remaining crystals from the side of the pan as these will cause the syrup to crystallise.

Increase the heat and boil until a rich golden colour. Allow to cool slightly. Working over sheets of baking paper, dip two forks into the syrup, join together then draw apart to form fine threads of toffee. Work quickly before the toffee sets and remember that it is very hot. When all the toffee has been used carefully lift the threads from the paper and place a little on top of each caramel custard.
Note: Do not attempt this if the weather is humid as the spun sugar will dissolve within moments of making. Prepare just before serving.

PEARS BELLE HÉLÈNE
Poires belle Hélène

2½ cups water
1 cup caster sugar
1 vanilla pod
4 pears, peeled
1½ cups vanilla ice-cream

PRALINE
½ cup caster sugar
1 tablespoon water
1 cup chopped nuts
oil for greasing

CHOCOLATE SAUCE
250 g dark or cooking chocolate
2 cups water
1 tablespoon sugar
few drops vanilla essence
3 tablespoons cream
10 g butter

Prepare syrup for pears. Combine water and sugar in a saucepan. Bring gradually to boil, stirring continually until sugar dissolves. Boil syrup for 1 minute and remove from heat. Immediately add vanilla pod. Cover and let syrup cool slowly so it becomes impregnated with vanilla flavour.

While syrup cools, make praline. Place sugar and water in a heavy-based saucepan. Slowly heat sugar until it begins to caramelise or turn golden. This should happen at 180°C (350°F). Stir in mixed chopped nuts and turn praline mixture onto a slightly oiled metal tray or shallow cake tin. Allow it to cool. When set, break up and crush into small pieces with a rolling pin.

Preheat oven to 190°C (375°F). Place pears in a shallow ovenproof dish. Remove and discard vanilla pod and pour syrup over pears. Poach pears in oven for 35 minutes basting and turning frequently to prevent pears browning and drying out. Cover and let them cool in syrup.

To prepare chocolate sauce: dissolve chocolate in water over a gentle heat. Stir in sugar and vanilla essence and cook sauce over a low heat for 20–25 minutes. Stir in cream and butter and keep sauce hot.

Just before serving, spread ice-cream over the bottom of a shallow serving dish. Drain pears and arrange on top. Serve with a bowl of hot chocolate sauce.
Serves 4

ORANGES IN GRAND MARNIER
Oranges au Grand Marnier

8 juicy, seedless oranges
¼ cup sugar
water
2 tablespoons Grand Marnier

Peel rind from 4 oranges, using a potato peeler or a sharp vegetable knife. Remove any white pith from it and shred peel finely. Put orange shreds into boiling water for 3 minutes, then drain.

Using a sharp knife, remove peel and pith from remaining oranges, catching drips of juice on a plate.

Put sugar in a pan with ½ cup cold water and stir over gentle heat until dissolved. Boil steadily without stirring until caramel is a rich golden brown. Remove from heat and add ½ cup hot water. Bring slowly back to the boil, then boil quickly to a syrupy consistency.

Add reserved orange juice and Grand Marnier and stir in orange shreds.

Arrange oranges in a serving dish and pour over sauce. Chill for several hours, spooning sauce over oranges occasionally. Provide a knife, fork and spoon for eating. *Note:* Alternatively, the oranges can be sliced, reassembled and secured with cocktail sticks.
Serves 8

MERINGUES IN CUSTARD
Oeufs à la neige

5 eggs
⅔ cup caster sugar
3 cups milk
few drops vanilla essence

Break eggs and place whites and yolks in separate bowls.

Add half the sugar to yolks and whisk them until they are creamy. Whisk egg whites until they are stiff, add remaining sugar and continue to whisk until meringue is very stiff.

Bring milk and vanilla to boil, reduce heat and drop 4 tablespoonfuls of meringue mixture into saucepan. Let meringues poach for 5 minutes on either side. Remove them with a draining spoon and place them on a clean cloth to dry.

Return milk to boil and gradually whisk it into egg yolk mixture. Return this mixture to saucepan and cook it over a low heat, stirring constantly with a wooden spoon until custard is smooth and coats spoon.

Strain custard and pour it into 4 individual serving dishes. Allow custard to cool. Place a poached meringue on top of each dish and chill in refrigerator for 1 hour before serving.
Serves 4

STRAWBERRY MERINGUE GÂTEAU
Vacherin aux fraises

4 egg whites
1 cup caster sugar
2–3 drops vanilla essence
450 g strawberries
1¼ cups thickened (double) cream
2 tablespoons Marsala
7 crystallised violets

CARAMEL
20 sugar lumps
1 tablespoon water

Preheat oven to 130°C (250°F). Place egg whites in a mixing bowl and beat well until stiff and glossy. It will save time and energy if you use an electric whisk.

Gradually add sugar, 1 tablespoon at a time, whisking well after each addition. When all sugar has been added, meringue should be very stiff.

Whisk in vanilla essence and fill a piping bag with meringue mixture.

Pipe a circle of meringue, 18 cm in diameter onto a sheet of non-stick baking paper. Pipe remaining meringue into 7 individual blocks, each 8 cm long and 4 cm wide.

Place meringue on a baking sheet and bake in oven for about 2 hours. Remove when dried out but not coloured. If meringue starts to colour, open oven door for a while.

To make caramel: place sugar and water in a saucepan and boil until you have a toffee-like sticky consistency.

Place cooled meringue base on a serving plate. Arrange meringue blocks around the sides to form a border, lying them on their sides. Stick them together with caramel and place them in position.

Wash and hull strawberries. Whip cream until thick and stiff and flavour it with Marsala. Fill a piping bag with cream and pipe some across the base. Pile strawberries up on top and pipe a large swirl of cream in centre, surrounded by smaller rosettes. Pipe a small swirl of cream between each of the meringue blocks on the edge of the plate. Decorate with crystallised violets and serve.
Serves 4

Oranges in Grand Marnier

Strawberry Meringue Gâteau

CRÈME CARAMEL

2 ¼ cups sugar
½ cup water
1 egg
1 egg yolk
3 tablespoons water
vanilla essence
2 ⅔ cups milk
***Spun Sugar** (see recipe)*
1 ¼ cups thickened (double) cream,
wbipped to serve

Bring ½ cup water and 1 cup sugar to boil in a heavy-based saucepan. Boil without stirring until mixture is a rich golden caramel colour. Pour caramel into 1 large mould, coating base and sides, or into 8 individual ramekin dishes. Set aside to cool.

Preheat oven to 180°C (350°F). Combine eggs, 1¼ cups sugar, 3 tablespoons water and vanilla essence. Heat milk, without boiling, and gradually whisk into egg mixture. Strain and pour into mould. Place mould in a baking tin half-filled with water and bake 40–50 mintes, or until set. Individual moulds will only take 20 minutes to cook. Test by inserting a butter knife into custard. If knife comes out clean, custard is set.

Chill thoroughly before turning out onto serving dish. Pour any caramel remaining in mould around dish and decorate with Spun Sugar if desired. Serve with whipped cream.
Serves 8

Crème Anglaise

CRÈME BRÛLÉE

2 tablespoons caster sugar
4 x 60 g egg yolks
1 teaspoon cornflour (cornstarch)
2 cups cream
2.5 cm vanilla or 1 teaspoon vanilla
* essence*
2 tablespoons caster sugar (extra)
2 tablespoons brown sugar

Beat sugar into egg yolks until mixture is pale yellow. Beat in cornflour, then gradually stir in cream, scalded with vanilla.

Pour mixture into the top of a double saucepan over hot water and stir slowly and continuously until custard thickens sufficiently to coat the back of a metal spoon. (Keep custard well under simmering point.)

Remove from heat and stir for 1–2 minutes to cool slightly. Strain into individual serving dishes. Chill well.

Just before serving, sprinkle combined extra caster sugar and brown sugar in a 3 mm layer over the top of custard. Place under a preheated grill until sugar melts and forms a golden toffee glaze. Serve immediately.
Serves 4

CRÈME ANGLAISE

6 × 60 g egg yolks
60 g caster sugar
600 mL milk
1 vanilla bean, split and scraped or 1
* teaspoon vanilla essence*

Whisk together egg yolks and sugar until pale in colour and sugar has dissolved.

Bring milk and vanilla bean to the boil then add to egg yolks in a slow steady stream, whisking constantly.

Pour into the top of a double boiler and cook over simmering water (never boiling) stirring with a wire whisk until custard thickens enough to coat the back of a metal spoon.

Remove from heat and cover closely with a sheet of dampened greaseproof (waxproof) paper to prevent a skin from forming. Use as required.
Makes approximately 2½ cups

COEUR À LA CRÈME

375 g cream-style cottage cheese
250 g cream cheese
1 tablespoon icing sugar, sifted
¼ cup thickened (double) cream, whipped
1 punnet raspberries or 250 g frozen and thawed
1 punnet fresh stawberries, to garnish

Cream together the 2 cheeses and fold in icing sugar and whipped cream. Line 6 Coeur à la Crème moulds with muslin and stand on a small tray. Spoon cheese mixture into moulds, smooth top and refrigerate overnight.

Unmould onto 6 dessert plates and remove muslin. Sift icing sugar over the top.

To make raspberry sauce: blend raspberries in processor. Sweeten to taste with icing sugar if desired. Spoon sauce around each Coeur à la Crème, placing strawberries to one side.

Note: Coeur à la Crème moulds are white, heart-shaped moulds available from cookware and department stores in the gourmet cookware section. Small ramekin moulds may be used as a substitute.

Serves 6

GRAND MARNIER SOUFFLÉ
Soufflé au Grand Marnier

melted butter
sugar
300 mL milk
2 tablespoons caster sugar
1 vanilla bean
75 g butter
50 g plain flour
6 × 60 g eggs, separated
1 extra egg white
1 tablespoon caster sugar
¼ cup Grand Marnier

Brush inside of a 1.5 litre soufflé dish with melted butter. Sprinkle a little sugar over the base and sides of the dish. Shake to remove excess. Collar line soufflé dish with greased paper.

Combine milk, sugar and vanilla in a saucepan and bring to the boil. Remove from heat and set aside to infuse flavours.

Melt butter in a medium-sized saucepan. Add flour and cook, stirring constantly for 1 minute. Remove from heat, gradually pour in strained milk stirring constantly until smooth. Return to heat and bring slowly to the boil.

Remove from heat, cool slightly and beat in egg yolks, 1 at a time. Add Grand Marnier. Place egg whites and salt into a clean, dry bowl and whisk until soft peaks form. Add caster sugar and continue whisking to form stiff peaks.

Fold a little egg white into the sauce then fold sauce into the remaining egg white, mixing until the sauce is of a uniform colour.

Spoon into the prepared dish and bake for 25 minutes or until well-risen and golden. Serve immediately.
Serves 4–6

Mini Chocolate Pots

MINI CHOCOLATE POTS
Petits pots au chocolat

125 g dark or cooking chocolate
2½ cups milk
2 eggs
2 egg yolks
2 tablespoons caster sugar
2 teaspoons rum
½ cup thickened (double) cream, whipped, to garnish

Preheat oven to 170°C (325°F).

Grate one square of chocolate for decoration. Place milk in a pan with remaining chocolate and heat to melt it.

Beat eggs, egg yolks and sugar together until light, then pour in hot but not boiling milk, stirring all the time. Stir in rum, then strain mixture into 6 individual ovenproof dishes.

Stand dishes in a roasting pan half filled with hot water, bake for 40–60 minutes or until custards are lightly set.

Serve hot or cold, decorated with whipped cream and grated chocolate.
Serves 6

CHESTNUT BAVAROIS
Bavarois Clermont

8 egg yolks
1 cup sugar
2 cups milk
2 teaspoons vanilla
2 tablespoons gelatine softened in ½ cup
*   cold water*
½ cup chestnut purée
600 mL thickened (double) cream, chilled
2 tablespoons dark rum

DECORATION
300 mL cream, whipped
fresh baby roses, crystallised

TO CRYSTALLISE ROSES
fresh baby roses, rinsed
1 egg white, lightly beaten
1 cup caster sugar

Rinse a 1.5 litre mould with water. Place in freezer to chill thoroughly.

Combine egg yolks with sugar and beat 10 minutes or until the mixture is thick and a pale lemon colour. Scald the milk and gradually add to the mixture, gently stirring. Transfer to the top of a double boiler and thicken over simmering water until the custard coats the back of a metal spoon. Remove from heat, cool slightly adding the softened gelatine, stir until dissolved.

Beat the chestnut purée with a little of the custard to form a smooth consistency. Stir into the remaining custard. Cool by standing in a basin of iced water (do not allow to set).

Beat cream only until soft peaks form, adding the rum. Both the custard and cream should be of the same consistency. Fold together. Pour the mixture into the mould and refrigerate for several hours until firm to the touch.

Loosen Bavarois from around the sides of the mould, invert onto a serving platter. Pipe whipped cream around the base of the Bavarois and decorate with the crystallised roses.

To crystallise roses: lightly paint the egg white onto the roses with a small paint brush. Dip the roses into the sugar, coating each petal. Shake off any excess. Arrange on greaseproof (waxproof) paper and set aside for several hours to dry.
Note: Chestnut Bavarois is a rich, mousse-like dessert set in a mould. Chestnut purée may be found at your supermarket and is sold in cans. In hot weather, add an extra tablespoon of gelatine.
Serves 6

CHOCOLATE COINTREAU MOUSSE
Mousse au chocolat et à la Cointreau

This mousse is very rich and a little goes a long way. It looks attractive served in small china pots and can then be stretched to serve 6 people.

250 g dark or cooking chocolate
3 tablespoons strong black coffee
20 g butter
1 tablespoon Cointreau
3 large eggs, separated
1 cup thickened (double) cream, whipped
*   for decoration*
Caraque (see recipe)

Break chocolate into small pieces and place with black coffee in a small bowl standing over a pan of hot water on gentle heat. Stir continuously until chocolate melts and becomes creamy. Cook gently for 2–3 minutes.

Remove bowl and stir in butter and Cointreau until butter dissolves. Cool slightly before beating in egg yolks.

Whisk egg whites until stiff and fold into chocolate mixture. Spoon into glasses or individual dishes and chill in refrigerator until set (about 1 hour). Serve decorated with a swirl of whipped cream and Caraque.
Serves 4–6

CARAQUE

50 g dark chocolate
knob of butter

Melt chocolate and butter over a double boiler. Allow to cool a little, then pour onto hard flat surface, such as marble or tiles. Spread it out quickly with a spatula. When chocolate is firm but not completely hard, scrape surface with a heavy kitchen knife or a spatula warmed in hot water.

Put the blade at 45° angle to the table and push. Chocolate will form long cylindrical curls which will break very easily so treat with care. Avoid touching Caraque if possible as the warmth of your hands will melt the chocolate very quickly. Use for decoration.

CRÊPES SUZETTE

2¼ cups flour
4 eggs
2 tablespoons sugar
pinch salt
few drops vanilla essence
2½ cups milk

ORANGE BUTTER
1 orange or 2 tangerines
½ cup caster sugar
100 g butter
⅓ cup orange liqueur e.g. Curacao or
*   Grand Marnier*
2 tablespoons oil

Sift flour into a large mixing bowl and stir in eggs one by one. Blend in sugar, salt and vanilla essence. Beat in milk gradually to form a smooth batter. Leave it to rest for 1 hour.

Grate rind and extract juice of orange.

Beat together caster sugar and butter with a wooden spoon until fluffy. Beat in orange rind and juice. Stir in ½ orange liqueur.

Lightly grease an omelette pan with a little oil. Pour in a large spoonful of batter and tilt pan so that an even circle is formed. Cook crêpe for 2 minutes on each side. Repeat until batter is used up, keeping cooked crêpes in a warm oven.

When all crêpes are cooked, spread each with some orange butter mixture. Fold then in 4 and arrange on a large warmed metal serving dish.

Just before serving, heat remaining liqueur in a small pan and pour it over crêpes. Ignite liqueur and serve immediately while burning.
Serves 6–8

APPLE CHARLOTTE
Charlotte de pommes

250 g unsalted butter
2 kg tart apples, peeled, cored and sliced
1 vanilla bean, split and scraped
1 cinnamon stick
1 tablespoon lemon juice
1 teaspoon lemon zest
180 g sugar or less, to taste
1 tablespoon Calvados or brandy
2 tablespoons apricot jam
12–14 slices white bread — crusts
*   removed, some cut into triangles for the*
*   base and some cut into rectangles for the*
*   sides*
Crème Anglaise (see recipe), for serving

Grease the bottom of a heavy pan with 150 g butter, add the sliced apples, vanilla bean, cinnamon stick, lemon juice and

Crêpes Suzette

zest. Place a piece of buttered paper over the apples and cover with a lid. Cook over a very low heat for 5 minutes until apples are soft.

Remove the cinnamon stick and vanilla bean. Add the sugar and stir over heat until the apple is thick and will barely fall from a spoon. (If the apple mixture is too soft the charlotte will collapse.) Add the Calvados and apricot jam. Simmer for 2–3 minutes.

Preheat oven to 200°C (400°F). Grease a charlotte mould and line the bottom with buttered greaseproof (waxproof) paper. Clarify the remaining butter. Dip the bread slices into the butter and line the bottom with the triangular pieces. Line the sides of the mould with the rectangular slices making sure they overlap. Spoon and pack the apple mixture into the mould and round the top slightly as it will shrink when cooked. Cover with remaining bread slices.

Dot the bread with a little butter. Place in the oven and bake for approximately 15 minutes or until the bread begins to brown. Reduce the heat to 180°C (350°F) and continue cooking for 40–50 minutes or until the charlotte is firm and very brown.

To serve hot allow the charlotte to stand unmoulded for 15 minutes.

Serve with Crème Anglaise.

Serves 6

93

RUM BABAS
Babas au rhum

1 teaspoon caster sugar
¼ cup warm milk
2 teaspoons dried yeast
1 cup + 2 tablespoons flour
pinch salt
2 eggs, beaten
4 tablespoons butter
⅔ cup thickened (double) cream, whipped
 to serve

RUM SYRUP

¼ cup honey
⅓ cup water
2 tablespoons dark rum
½ teaspoon grated lemon rind

In a bowl, dissolve sugar in milk and sprinkle over yeast. Put in a warm place and leave to ferment for 20 minutes or until frothy.

Sieve flour and salt in a warm bowl. Make a well in centre of flour and add yeast and milk, beaten eggs and butter. Mix well and knead dough until it is smooth and elastic.

Cover with a cloth and leave to prove in a warm place for 30 minutes.

Preheat oven to 200°C (400°F).

Half-fill 8 × 150 mL pudding basins or dariole moulds with dough. Cover with a cloth and leave them to rise for 20 minutes, or until the moulds are ⅔ full.

Bake babas in oven for 20 minutes or until golden brown.

A few minutes before babas are ready, prepare syrup. Place honey, water, rum and grated lemon rind in a saucepan. Heat gently, stirring continually, until ingredients are well-blended.

Turn babas out onto a rack placed in a baking dish. Prick each baba with a fine skewer and baste them with rum syrup. Serve decorated with whipped cream.
Serves 8

NOEL LOG
Bûche de Nöel

1 Genoese Sponge
100 g cooking chocolate, melted and cooled
1 tablespoon instant coffee, dissolved in
 boiling water
3 tablespoons rum
2 tablespoons apricot jam, combined with
2 tablespoons water and strained

MERINGUE MUSHROOMS
1 egg white
2 tablespoons caster sugar

DECORATION
cocoa powder
2 tablespoons almond flakes
holly leaves

GENOESE SPONGE
4 x 55 g eggs
½ cup caster sugar
vanilla essence, to taste
1 cup flour, sifted
120 g unsalted butter, melted and cooled

BASIC BUTTERCREAM
3 egg yolks
3 tablespoons icing sugar, sifted
200 g unsalted butter, softened

To prepare Genoese Sponge: whisk eggs and sugar in the top of a double boiler over simmering water. Beat 5–10 minutes, until pale and creamy in texture. Remove from heat and continue beating until volume has trebled (10–20 minutes). Add vanilla essence. Using a large metal spoon, fold in flour gradually. Quickly and lightly fold in melted butter.

Pour batter into a greased and paper-lined 22 cm spring-form tin or 2 sandwich tins. Bake in preheated oven at 180°C (350°F).

Pour batter into a greased 22 cm spring-form tin or 2 sandwich tins. Bake in preheated oven at 180°C (350°F).

To make the mushrooms: whisk egg white until it forms firm peaks; sift over ½ the sugar and whisk until mixture is stiff and shiny. Sift over remaining sugar in 2 stages, and fold it into mixture. Using a plain nozzle, pipe stalks and different-sized circles for the caps onto aluminium foil. Bake at 150°C (300°F) for 15–20 minutes. Peel off paper carefully and cool on a rack.

To prepare Buttercream: blend all ingredients until smooth; chill for 20 minutes. Set aside 4 tablespoons Buttercream; combine the rest with the melted chocolate and coffee.

Sprinkle sponge with rum. Cover it with ⅓ chocolate Buttercream and roll it up. Cut 1 end of roll straight and the other at a sharp angle. Brush all surfaces with warmed apricot jam. Smooth some unflavoured Buttercream over each end of the roll.

Using a star nozzle on a large piping bag, fill with remaining chocolate Buttercream. Pipe uneven lines along the roll, to give a bark-like effect. Using a small piping bag with a narrow plain nozzle, pipe concentric, chocolate cream circles on the plain cream ends.

Sprinkle cocoa on meringue caps; attach the stalks to the caps with Buttercream. Place the mushrooms on the log. Garnish with almonds and holly leaves. Chill for 2–3 hours or overnight and serve.
Serves 8

VANILLA ICE-CREAM
Glace vanille

600 mL milk
6 x 60 g egg yolks
150 g caster sugar
300 mL cream
1 vanilla bean, split in ½ lengthwise

In a saucepan combine milk with ½ sugar and the vanilla bean and bring to boil. Remove from heat and set aside to infuse the flavours.

Beat the egg yolks with remaining sugar for 8 minutes or until creamy and almost white. Remove vanilla bean from milk. Pour ½ boiling milk onto egg mixture, very gradually and whisking constantly. Return to saucepan with remaining milk.

Cook mixture stirring over very low heat until it coats the back of a metal spoon.

Remove from heat and continue stirring for 2 minutes. Add the cream and when combined pour into a deep metal tray. Cool and then freeze.

When ice crystals start to form 4 cm in from edge of tray, transfer the ice-cream to a bowl and beat with a fork. Return to metal tray and freeze. Cover with freezer wrap and place in a sealed freezer bag.
Makes 1 litre

LEMON SORBET
Sorbet citron

125 g caster sugar
4 lemons
1¾ cups water
1 egg white

In a small saucepan combine sugar, grated rind of 2 lemons and water.

Stir over a low heat until sugar has dissolved. Bring to boil and cook, without stirring, for 6 minutes. Cool and strain. Add lemon juice from 4 lemons. Whisk egg whites to form soft peaks and fold into the syrup. Pour into a deep metal tray and freeze.

Refrigerate 10 minutes before serving.
Makes 1 litre

Index

ACKNOWLEDGEMENTS

The publisher would like to thank the following companies for their generous assistance with cookware and tableware during the photography of this book:
Doulton Tableware for tableware (pages 30, 32, 37, 39, 41, 51, 57, 84, 87)
Hale Imports for Pillivuyt, cookware and tableware (pages 8, 9, 13, 15, 17, 23, 31, 32, 45, 48, 59, 68, 70, 80, 81)
Johnson's Overalls for cookwear (pages 8, 9, 15, 16, 26, 35, 63, 89)
Lifestyle Imports (page 73)

Printed in Singapore